Risen Today

RISEN TODAY

Bernard Thorogood

SCM PRESS LTD

British Library Cataloguing in Publication Data

Thorogood, Bernard
Risen today.
1. Jesus Christ—Resurrection
I. Title
232'.5 BT481

ISBN 0–334–02299–1

First published 1986
by SCM Press Ltd,
26–30 Tottenham Road, London N1 4BZ

Typeset at The Spartan Press Ltd,
Lymington, Hants
and printed in Great Britain by
Richard Clay Ltd
Bungay, Suffolk

Contents

Preface

One of the primary qualities of the witness of the apostles was that they should testify to the resurrection of Jesus. It is still a central theme of the church. It stands firmly in our statements of faith. Yet it puzzles and disturbs some Christians while baffling those not accustomed to the language of faith. Recent controversies have added to feelings of uncertainty but also perhaps to our readiness to speak of this dimension of our faith. It is within that context that these chapters have been written. For it is my conviction that the apostolic tradition is ours, that we too are witnesses of the resurrection, and that this is the root of our fellowship as the church of Christ today.

But it is not a topic which I can approach in a theoretical way, nor just as biblical study. Both those approaches are no doubt possible. I have taken the New Testament evidence as the closest we can get to the historical facts, and I have not searched out a history behind the sources. Rather I have attempted to see how the narratives of the resurrection point us to ways in which the risen Christ appeared then and approaches us now, so that we may know him and hear him.

So the mood in which I have written is one of meditation on the living Christ in our world. He is a reality of faith, both a searching test of our lives and a forgiving word in those who love and accept us. He is as near to us as to Peter and Cleopas and Thomas and Mary. We stand in their shoes, wondering, reading, glimpsing messengers of grace, and then we know that the Lord is here, in the breaking of bread or the word of peace or the many signs of God in the midst of us.

Yet the risen Christ is always beyond us, not imprisoned by our dimensions of time or thought. So we look at the meaning of his presence for the church and for ourselves as we plod or skip through our brief years, assured that the context in which we live is the eternal dimension. The Lord who is risen and for ever is the very one who is immediate, personal, speaking my name.

I come from the Reformed tradition of church life and serve the United Reformed Church. Not given very much to credal statements, we nevertheless hold firmly to the reality of the resurrection. My own awareness has grown through people. I rejoice in the memory of pastors who have shared the experience of Easter: George Douglas Evans, who led me through my teens by patient, humble ministry. Then, representing Christians of another culture, in Polynesia, Pastor Eliaba, a wise elder for a young missionary. Gratitude for companions in the Emmaus Road.

1

Apostolic Witness

In the most vigorous and powerful opening of his letter, the apostle John pours out his conviction about the basis of faith.

> It was there from the beginning; we have heard it; we have seen it with our own eyes; we have looked upon it, and felt it with our own hands; and it is of this we tell. Our theme is the word of life. This life was made visible; we have seen it and bear our testimony; we here declare to you the eternal life which dwelt with the Father and was made visible to us (I John 1.1–2).

To speak in such terms is a unique apostolic confession. All those who walked and talked with Jesus Christ had heard and touched and seen the very creative energy of God, the eternal expression of God's nature. That was the claim. On that rested the dynamic of the apostles' preaching. Here was the assurance which could withstand both intellectual questioning and active persecution. What you have seen, heard and touched is not something you can deny. Here also was the authority of the apostles among the spreading Christian community, not an authority of power or titles or constitutions but of first-hand knowledge of Christ.

If only we could write like John, what a difference that would make to our Christian witness! When preachers sometimes say 'Come to Jesus', what do they mean? How can we meet a historical figure? The distance between us and Jesus is not only two thousand years but the vast culture gap involved. We read of New Testament times and the great influences that surrounded people in Palestine, the belief in spirits, the limited knowledge of the natural world, the pervasive but disapproved Greek philosophy, the whole Jewish background of sacrifice and law, the tribal heritage, the coded languages – and we know that our lives are a long way from Jesus.

It is no answer to us that we can see Jesus portrayed in drama and film with great realism and vividness. We may understand the story much better in that way, but we meet an actor and not Jesus. Historical drama has become very highly polished in modern television, and I marvel at the re-creation of Dickens and Trollope, with every drawing-room detail perfectly judged and every landscape devoid of all signs of electric cable. Even the cows look Victorian. But it remains a stage and I am in the stalls, and when the show ends, my world and that world are separated again. I do not really meet Jesus that way.

Nor is it an answer to say that biblical scholarship can expose Jesus to us in a full and living way. I am not among those who love to criticize the biblical scholars as being destructive of faith, for I think they have done a great service to all thinking Christians by revealing the character and essential meaning of those words and documents. Of course, if we still retain a view of scripture which dismisses the writers as only mouthpieces for a divine composition, then any human enquiry into the origins of the documents is both a wasted effort and an improper delving into mystery. But scholarship and research have helped those who recognize the Bible as a complex work, and its writers as limited by their language and their sources. What scholarship cannot do is to bring Jesus more clearly before us than do the books themselves.

Can we meet Jesus? The answer in this book is that we can, and that the way God has opened for us is through the resurrection and the ascension.

The apostles were witnesses of the resurrection. In a sense that was the qualification which allowed them to become preachers to the world. At a time when we today hear a good deal of questioning about the resurrection, for it fits uneasily into our scientific cast of mind, it is good to remember that it was this reality which alone stimulated the courageous witness of the very first church. Without it the disciples would surely have slipped back into a minor sect of Judaism, fondly recalling their great prophet but with no power to turn the world upside down. When we ask awkward questions about resurrection (as honesty compels us to do), we can do so from the assurance that the biblical evidence is solid. There are two central facts to which the evangelists give witness with unanimity: the tomb was empty; Jesus was alive. Much else remains indistinct. The order of events is a little shaky. We may take Paul's list in I Corinthians 15 as a basis:

> that he was raised to life on the third day according to the scriptures; and that he appeared to Cephas and afterwards to the twelve. Then he appeared to over five hundred of our brothers at once, most of whom are still alive, though some have died. Then he appeared to James and afterwards to all the apostles (I Cor. 15.4–7).

That list contains five appearances, and those do not precisely agree with any of the four Gospel records. We shall probably conclude that none of the records is fully comprehensive and each gives one view of a series of events in which different people shared.

Again, we are left in some doubt as to the appearance of the tomb itself on that Sunday morning. John tells in detail of the grave-wrappings being there, but no body; Luke and Matthew make no mention of the cloths but tell of the angel; while Mark writes of a youth wearing a white robe. At these points we can acknowledge uncertainty. But on the two great issues there was no uncertainty. The grave where Jesus was laid to rest on Friday afternoon was empty on Sunday. From that Sunday those who knew and loved Jesus saw, heard and touched him, the very Word of life, as he came to them. The writers of the New Testament were not absorbed, as we are, by the question 'How did it happen?' We find that fascinating. Theories abound. Today people meditate on nuclear physics and the Turin shroud and astonishing effects of holograms. But that is just speculation which I find profitless. The 'how' is missing from the records and it is beyond us. It is far better to think about the meaning of the risen Christ for ourselves and our world.

The grave was empty. This has many implications. It tells us that there was no full stop, no final curtain to the life story of Jesus, no sacred relics to be honoured by future generations, no way for Jews and Roman authorities to extinguish the new faith, and no finality in physical death. For us, a tomb spells corruption. But the Gospel is good news about life from the very grave itself. Jesus was alive. The utter disbelief of the apostles is recorded as a vivid sign of the strangeness of the happening. The unevenness of the accounts tells us that there was mystery surrounding the appearances. Yet the only way we can read these vivid stories is as evidence that the very same Jesus who was known and honoured, who was nailed to the cross and buried in the tomb, who was Rabbi, Messiah and friend, this Jesus and none other met the disciples with a message of life.

On these basic elements the witnesses agree. We have the five accounts in the Gospels and First Corinthians, probably written at very different places over a period of perhaps fifty years, yet with total agreement on the two essentials. There can be very few events of similar antiquity about which the same strength of evidence can be gathered. As we live out our faith in the apostolic tradition, we can have confidence in this tremendous element of the Christian creed. But within this tradition we can probe a little further. The accounts of the resurrection appearances contain some surprising features and are not altogether what we might expect.

2

The Stranger

For the inner group of disciples, the men and women who had travelled with Jesus during his ministry, he was the most familiar figure. His appearance, the way he walked and turned to listen, the tones of his voice and the combinations of gesture and emphasis all must have composed a well-loved picture in their minds. So when Jesus appeared to them after Easter we would expect instant recognition. We do not find it. In every case there is a hesitation, a question-mark, which is recorded. We can attribute a good deal of this to utter amazement: it just cannot be true. But that would not explain how the same non-recognition is recorded in the later episodes.

Who is this Jesus, both known and unknown? Yes, it is the same Jesus, for the scars are evidence for those who needed it. But there is a distinction between the Jesus who died and the Jesus who appeared to the disciples. I see it as the strangeness of the process by which the same Lord, Jesus Christ, Son of God, was being freed from the limitations of incarnation. In ways that are not known to us and not now discoverable to our scientific analysis, Jesus was being lifted beyond the physical dimensions of the body, a process which was completed at the ascension. The movement of Jesus into closed rooms and his removal from the sight of the apostles suggest such a change, while the emphasis on food and eating is given to us to emphasize that there was indeed a resurrection of the body.

Here I want to concentrate particularly on the non-recognition factor because it leads me to see how Jesus made himself known. Jesus was revealed in a particular and not a general way. He did not walk the streets of Jerusalem, with all the crowds shouting, 'Praise the Lord, here is the crucified one.' The street crowd, the Temple authorities and the Roman military did not see him. Nor did he resume his old life with the disciples as constant companion and teacher. In this there is a distinction from the story of Lazarus, who appears to have resumed his old position in the Bethany home after the events in John 11 (see John 12.2). Jesus was not 'at home' in this sense with the disciples. He came to them at his own times and in his own ways. This was surely a part of the training which the disciples needed before Jesus left them as a physical person. It was a stage in their preparation, for they had to come to terms with a faithful pilgrimage without that figure leading them on.

When Jesus stood before them, there was a question about who he was. Mary Magdalene thought he was the gardener (John 20.15), although he was the person she knew and loved above all others. The eleven disciples had to be reassured by the word of peace repeated (John 20.20). More surprising, two disciples could walk along the Emmaus Road, discuss the events and listen to a tutorial on the Old Testament by the Lord without recognizing him. 'Something held their eyes from seeing who it was' (Luke 24.16). Luke then records the meeting with the eleven and the need for Jesus to show the scars and to eat a piece of fish in order that they might be fully convinced of his reality (Luke 24.36–43). In Galilee Jesus met the fishermen. He stood on the beach, 'but the disciples did not know that it was Jesus' (John 21.4). Even when the recognition came, there was still a strange distance between them. 'None of them dared to ask, "Who are you?" They knew it was the Lord' (John 21.12). But if they knew, why should such a question arise? Finally, at the end of Matthew's Gospel, when all these events had taken place and the last act of the drama was upon them, the eleven made their way to Galilee, to the mountain already arranged by Jesus. 'When they saw him they fell prostrate before him, though some were doubtful' (Matthew 28.17).

It strains belief that eleven men who knew Jesus so intimately should not know him if, in every respect, he was the same in all physical characteristics. A further indication of the changing presence of Christ is the phrase he used in the garden to Mary: 'Do not cling to me, for I have not yet ascended to the Father' (John 20.17). This suggests more than the good teacher who refuses to be paternalistic. It is much more the warning not to cling to the flesh because it is improper to do so, or because that kind of human clinging is no longer possible. Something had changed. The death had been real enough, agonizing, completed, and with that there was an ending; the ending not of the work of Christ or the power of Christ, but of his fully earthly, physical presence in the midst of human society. He was moving towards the further change which we know as ascension when the physical presence would be left altogether, and the life of infinite glory would flood the world. If the self-emptying and the glorifying of Christ described by Paul in Philippians may be thought of as a parabola, a downward and upward movement, then the resurrection appearances are at the turning point where both downward and upward are present.

This is hard to describe because there is mystery here. The incarnation is a mystery. We do not fully understand how the majesty and eternity of God entered into our human framework, with all its weakness, risk and limitation. Yet this is the testimony. The body of Jesus was a real body, like ours, and his death was equally real. All the theories which attempted to wish away that reality and to show Jesus passing through the world with the appearance but not the reality of flesh were rightly judged to be false teaching. Luke's Gospel is our plainest testimony. 'Why do questionings arise in your minds? Look at my hands and my feet. It is I myself. Touch me and see; no ghost has flesh and bones as you can see that I have' (Luke 24.38–39). Paul wrestled with the nature of the body which was raised, and in I Corinthians 15 we have the almost poetical verses in which Paul described how 'all flesh is not the same flesh; there is flesh of men, flesh of beasts, birds and fishes – all different. There are heavenly bodies and earthly bodies; and the splendour of the heavenly bodies is one thing, the splendour of the earthly bodies another . . . So it is with the resurrection of the dead. What is sown in the earth as a perishable thing is raised imperishable. Sown in humiliation, it is raised in glory; sown in weakness, it is raised in power; sown as an animal body, it is raised as a spiritual body' (I Cor. 15.39–44). So Christ as the second Adam wears this new clothing as he leads his people past the gates of death. God provides the presence which is needed for our salvation: both the man in weakness, vulnerability and pain; and the man who is beyond all three, the man who is in heaven.

The words used here by Paul, humiliation, weakness and animal, provide a stark contrast to our modern Western thinking about the nature of our bodies. The endless advertising campaigns teach us all to regard the body as potentially beautiful and therefore to be pampered. The keep-fit specialists also promote, in repetitious colourful books, the exercises that will make our bodies Hollywood-handsome. We are part of a privileged enclave. These were the attributes of an old aristocracy, far removed from the struggles of the ordinary people. So we need to think back into the biblical world if we are to capture the flavour of the apostolic message. They were not saying that physical bodies were repellent or deformed or to be ashamed of. Rather, they looked at the body as the vehicle for what is more precious, the personality. They saw a person, a soul, shining through the eyes and speaking through the lips. And they were realists who knew that eyes and lips wither with the years. They lived at a period of short life-expectancy, when women were old and bent at forty, when many infants died and when little could be done to alleviate pain. In this instance the biblical background differs from the ancient Greek culture which, for the privileged, could present the glory of the physical body. Jewish tradition very rarely rejoiced in that aspect of creation, and this may be why the Bible tells us so little of the appearance of people. Yet Jesus came to us, 'bearing the human likeness, revealed in human shape' (Phil. 2.8), subject to pain and decay, flesh of our flesh.

We can interpret this mystery in terms of limitation. The man Jesus was limited to a very local spot on this earth and to a few years out of the span of history. He was limited to one language and culture out of many. He was limited in his knowledge of geography and astronomy and all the sciences. He was limited by the weariness of the body and the need to rest. This is involved in incarnation. These limitations were beginning to fall away at the time of the resurrection appearances, and perhaps this is what made Jesus less knowable, more remote. From the time of the ascension, all the limitations fall away and Jesus Christ, with the Father and the Holy Spirit one God, fills all the universe with purpose, hope and love.

3

The Seeker

Jesus did not leave his friends. Knowing that the events of Friday must have shattered their confidence, leaving them bereft, leaderless, uncertain, the Lord met them; and each meeting was for the renewal of their trust in him. The initiative lay with him. There was no way now for them to follow him, in the physical sense, from place to place, and keep him in view. So Jesus chose the times and places. The familiar places drew them together, the Galilee hills and the upper room in Jerusalem; there Jesus appeared and, in spite of the non-recognition, made himself known. This initiative shows how well Jesus knew his friends and their individual needs. At each point he showed himself in ways that corresponded to the experience and faith already there, so that conviction could be complete.

In the garden, in the early morning, Mary Magdalene was frightened and baffled, so that when Jesus stood before her she did not know him, not dreaming of so tremendous a possibility. Jesus spoke her name and recognition was complete. He was appealing to the personal relationship which is evident in the Gospels, a deep thanksgiving for acceptance and a deep devotion to Rabboni, Teacher. It is not fanciful to see in that relationship the God-given route by which Mary was reborn, in which she discovered the way to a good life and to a love which enriched human personality. That had been the gift of the Lord to her. Her name, in the voice of Jesus, was an affirmation of all that was best in her. 'You are not in a class of the despised, not labelled with a brand name of uselessness, not on the shelf as merchandise – you are the person I know and care for.'

In the Upper Room the word was 'Peace'. We may take it as a customary greeting, quite casual and ordinary. Or we may see it as a signal or declaration. The depth of the word was certainly part of the teaching of Jesus, so it must have had various shades of meaning for the disciples. 'Peace is my parting gift to you, my own peace, such as the world cannot give' (John 14.27). This was a distinctive claim and a comfort for those who would be utterly dismayed by the crucifixion and for all who, in Christ's name, would face a storm of opposition in later years. On the day of resurrection, the word was a promise fulfilled. What Jesus had offered at the table in the Upper Room he now could reveal to them, so that this peace of heart, the peace of victory over death, the peace which could not come through law or alliances or morality or tradition but was based on the very character of God, could now shine in the same room and fill troubled hearts and minds.

But the word did not stand on its own. It was accompanied by the sight of the scars. At this point we are almost overwhelmed by the mystery of Christ. Our wounded God! Jesus came to the disciples as the one who endured pain, whose flesh had been torn by human force, who was as threatened by the nails as we would be. This is a firm statement of incarnation, in which the ultimate authority and creative power of God is united with the fragility, frailty and uncertainty of the human condition. There is no greater wonder than this in our faith. In the many wonders of ancient religion there are frequent appearances of gods in human form, a host of mythical god-men, goddess-women and even god-animals. Yet there is always the sense that they can escape the last indignity and return to the home of the gods. That is, after all, what we would expect. Why would a divine being suffer the worst horrors of execution? We can only answer that the calling of the divine will in him led him to offer himself as a lamb to the slaughter. So the scars became the marks of obedience and love.

> The other gods were strong; but Thou wast weak;
> They rode, but Thou didst stumble to a throne;
> But to our wounds God's wounds alone can speak
> and not a god has wounds but Thou alone.
>> Edward Shillito (1872-1948), *Jesus of the Scars*

Thus the scars lead us, as they led the disciples, to recognize one who is properly called not only 'Rabboni' but 'My Lord and my God' (John 20.28).

The next recognition sign – or rather the sign of Christ's approach – is the conversation on the Emmaus Road with Cleopas and friend. Jesus joined them for what sounds like a long walk on a familiar road. He rebuked them for their dullness in not connecting the empty tomb with the promise of new life, and then began to interpret for them the scripture passages which pointed to victory over death. Jesus was claiming continuity in God's revelation; the promise and the fulfilment of the promise were both God's gift of light to the people who walked in darkness. He was helping two puzzled men to start with what they knew – the scripture – and move on to the startling reality that scripture is but a small foretaste of God's saving mercy. The use of scripture was more than a comfort and assurance; it was also the means of understanding the fulfilment. A similar point is made in Acts 8 when Philip expounded to the Ethiopian the text of Isaiah 53. We are led to the meaning of Christ and the resurrection through the preparatory glimpses of the prophets and the discipline of the people of God.

But they did not recognize Jesus until they reached home and welcomed him to the supper table. Then at the moment when he took up the loaf and broke off a piece, they knew him. Vivid in their memory was the supper at which Jesus had taught them, had shared bread and wine with them, and prayed to the Father that they might be held in unity and love. In the action they recognized him, and not, so far as we can tell, from any accompanying words. This was the way in which Jesus chose to be recognized. It reminds us that the simple action is often the most vivid witness which declares who we are. While we may write a host of satisfying details about ourselves in a *curriculum vitae*, these are studied outlines of a career, and tell relatively little about the sort of people we really are. When we act spontaneously or habitually, without any self-justification, others can glimpse our personality. It may be in this instance that Jesus was acting as the father of the family would, breaking the loaf at the head of the table, and recognition may have been in that fatherly position. Or it may have been a direct reference to the Last Supper. We are reminded of the holiness of bread, the blessing of the breaking and the communion of the eating, and we thank God that the risen Lord is known in this way.

Turning to John's account, the scene moves to Galilee and the fishermen on the lake. Jesus is on the beach. He sees the tiredness of the disciples and their failure to make a catch, and comes to the rescue. In following his direction the net is filled and it is John himself who recognizes the Lord in that moment of wonder. Peter reacts swiftly, leaving the others to row the laden boat ashore, and perhaps questioning why he could not wait to lend a hand. Then, on the beach, Jesus invites them to a barbecue breakfast and all questions are silenced as the familiar hands pass bread and fish. Jesus is known in the actions of friendship, seeing the disappointment of his friends and their hunger, and meeting both. This was not giving in to the early temptation to turn stones into bread, a miracle which tempted Jesus to gain a crowd and a crown the easy way, but rather a family matter in which the care of Jesus was to be demonstrated with simplicity.

Finally, all four Gospel writers tell us of Jesus making himself known as he calls the disciples to a great commission. The four accounts are rather different. In Mark the verses (16.14–20) only uncertainly belong to the Gospel, but the manuscripts in which they appear do carry weight and cannot be dismissed. We are given the words of Jesus: 'Go forth to every part of the world, and proclaim the good news to the whole creation' (v.15). The words are followed by a promise of miraculous powers. Luke does not end his Gospel with these words, but he starts the book of Acts in a very similar way. 'You will receive power when the Holy Spirit comes upon you; and you will bear witness for me in Jerusalem, and all over Judaea and Samaria, and away to the ends of the earth' (Acts 1.8). So Luke clearly focusses attention on the beginning of the missionary story rather than the ending of the Gospel story, and the verse with its geographical detail actually provides the outline of the book that follows. Matthew gives us the commission very much as a Gospel summary. His wording sounds as though it is a formula very often repeated, and this may indicate that in parts of the infant church this was used as a blessing at the end of worship. 'Go forth therefore and make all nations my disciples; baptize men everywhere in the name of the Father and the Son and the Holy Spirit, and teach them to observe all that I have commanded you. And be assured, I am with you always, to the end of time' (Matthew 28.18–20). We have the sense of a much more formal stage of church life in that version. John also has a commissioning at the end of the Gospel, but it is very different in character. It is a conversation between Jesus and Peter in which the threefold denial of Jesus before the cross becomes a threefold affirmation of Peter's commitment, and concludes with a repeated 'Follow me' (John 21.15–23). Jesus is still a commanding figure, but also a loving friend who sees Peter's distress of heart and rescues him with a particular calling, to 'feed my sheep'. It is worth noting the contrast here with Matthew 16.18, where Jesus calls Peter the rock on which the church is built. In John's Gospel Peter is very unrock-like, and needs both correction and reassurance; the final commission is a call to serve and cherish the brethren, not to rule an institution. Here again the Matthew words seem to reflect a more formalized period of church thought. But in all four writers the last words of Jesus are a statement of God's continuing purpose through his followers, words of great authority.

Here are seven ways in which Jesus showed himself: by naming, by the peace, by the scars, by scripture, by breaking bread, by friendship and by authority to commission others. In each case Jesus took the initiative, seeking his friends, leading them to a fuller belief and demonstrating the continuity of his life, character and purpose. No doubt Jesus could have declared the resurrection in many other ways. As John wrote: 'There is much else that Jesus did. If it were all to be recorded in detail, I suppose the whole world could not hold the books that would be written' (John 21.25). These incidents, however, offer us good ground for seeking the seeking Christ. After the ascension the Lord was free of the limits of the place and the date. He could make himself known to people of every age and every culture, and the initiative is still with him. But every point at which Christ is alive, seeking us, is also a point where our response is sought, our acceptance welcomed, our faith deepened. Christ is for the world. He may come to us in the voices of friends and in the beauty of creation – there is no limit to his presence among us, and Christians who have erected narrow channels for him to meet humanity have done a disservice to the mystery of God. But of all the means of meeting Jesus, it is people who are his highway. Since God came to us in a person it is a proper interpretation for us to say that God is personal and is speaking to us most of all in people.

We are confirmed in this by Paul's understanding of the risen Christ.

By baptism we were buried with him, and lay dead, in order that, as Christ was raised from the dead in the splendour of the Father, so also we might set our feet upon the new path of life (Romans 6.4).

Baptized into union with him, you have all put on Christ as a garment (Galatians 3.26).

The life I now live is not my life, but the life which Christ lives in me, and my present bodily life is lived by faith in the Son of God (Galatians 2.20).

The secret is this: Christ in you, the hope of glory to come (Colossians 1.27).

This conviction that the living Christ lives in and through his people is the basis of Paul's understanding of the church. It is not idealizing the sinful realities of Corinth or London or wherever, but looking behind our partial witness to the one who promised to be with us to the end of the age. We know that the resurrection is a reality because Jesus approaches us and calls us and heals us through women and men in whom the Holy Spirit has worked the miracle of grace.

4

I Called You by Name

It must be one of the most frightening experiences to wake up after an accident and not know who you are. No address, no parents, no bank account, no familiar road home, no favourite food, no memory of beauty seen and heard. Just a blank sheet of mental paper. That is the image of those who do not know their true identity, or, knowing it, spurn it and adopt a fantasy, Walter Mitty existence. How do we know our real identity as human beings? We know our animal, physical life through our senses, for we trust our eyes and ears and nerves to provide the extent of our physical being. For some people that has been enough. They have given such omnipotence to the senses and have so down-graded thought, imagination, hope, caring love, language, that present sensation is all that counts.

That is a small minority, for most people know that life is more than a full stomach and warm skin. We know that an animal life is wholly inadequate to account for human nature. The poet Coleridge once said, 'To be an animal is something the really bad man cannot hope to be.' Always we are something more, and therefore more guilty than an animal. But also more blessed. We live in a physical world, but our relationship to that world is complex. Our bodies can be bruised or pampered, we can heal and we can maim with exceptional power, we can cower before the thunderstorm or create our own thunder, we can replant a desert or make a new desert. We can serve the creation or try to twist it to our own purposes. Then there is a whole world which is not measured by our senses. We all know of the world of dreams, the world of love and hate, the world of logic and the realm of planning for the future. There is a cosmos of ideas, a Milky Way of guilt and a solar system of mutual respect. As we inhabit those worlds we ask, 'Who are we, this strange hybrid which rules a planet?'

The question is posed with even greater force by those who are torn from their roots. We think of orphans or deserted children in war who are caught up in the great movements of refugees and never discover what happened to their parents. There are those who are so emancipated from their origins that they have become the slaves of fashion and move restlessly from one craze to the next. Or we can remember those who are utterly dominated by a cruel parent so that they become virtual prisoners, with no personal identity. This situation has become more common in our mobile, urban society, where fewer people are grounded in a family background, many have no real friends, where technology or the rat race seems to reduce human personality and people are all too often judged by their bank balance. Am I just a number in a computer memory bank?

Into this real world Jesus comes and calls us by name as he called Mary in the garden. In all her surprise, distress, fear and loneliness she heard a familiar voice say 'Mary', and she was able to respond, 'My Master'. It is a gift of God in the person of Christ to call us by name so that, in all our confusion, we may recognize our true position in the world.

The witness of the apostles to the life of Jesus emphasizes that each person he met was treated as a
responsible child of God with great potential, whatever
handicap was being carried. The 'child of God' element
was crucial. Men and women were in a special relationship to the creator of the universe – whether they knew it
or not – and therefore belonged both to this visible world
and to the realm of the eternal spirit. This affirmation was
made in every prayer of Christ, in the promise of the
Holy Spirit, in the teaching about worry, in many
parables of the Kingdom. It is an affirmation acted in the
way Jesus dealt with a Roman centurion and a dying thief
on a cross. It is heard in the calling of the Twelve to be
co-workers with Christ. It is supremely evident in the
word of Jesus for God, Abba, Father. So we know that we
are participants in more than one level of existence, so
that the animal life never fully satisfies us and 'our hearts
are restless until they find their rest' in the Father. But
Jesus also treated people as responsible. They had to
make choices, often testing choices, for themselves, and
were not to be pushed or dragged or compelled into a
style of life and a way of worship. When he challenged
people, 'Follow me', they had to decide how to respond,
and many turned away. His whole life was such a
question posed to his contemporaries, and their answer
was, 'Crucify him.' So while 'child of God' signifies
dependence on the ultimate love and authority behind
the whole creation, everyone is given sufficient autonomy to make all the key responses in adult life which
determine whether we obey the truth that has been given
to us. And each is with great potential, whatever the
present handicap may be. If it is paralysis, then there is a
possibility of walking; if it is wealth, then that can be
given away; if it is sin, then there is a way of forgiveness.

Jesus calls us by this name, each one of us, so that we may know our place in the marvellous universe, and trust that each one has potential, however depressed or painful our present experience. We can respond, with Mary, 'My Master', because we have glimpsed the whole story of Christ, leading to the cross and the empty tomb. To be addressed and to respond is an aspect of the healing work of Christ, so that we may be able to accept who we are. Many of us live with strange images of ourselves and would wish to bear another name. We are often torn apart by such inner confusion. We want to be heroes, but are cowards; athletic, but are clumsy; good parents, but are irritable; and some of us are pastors when our hearts are full of anger; lovers when we are filled with fear; teachers when we know nothing but a textbook.

The resurrection means that Jesus is alive. His way of addressing us by name today is through many people, but here we note two: the first which comes to all of us, and the second which is a particular ministry to people in special need.

We are called by name through our closest family. That is where we are given a name at birth and perhaps other names as we go along through childhood. It is where we are known most intimately, where we reveal most (though never all) of our character. It is where, in a Christian context, we are cared for but not dominated, corrected and loved, held in respect but never flattered, because the worst as well as the best in us is accepted. That is the security of being named by those close to us. Of course a great deal happens to deny this. The Christian family has been no beautiful model which all other religions and epochs can look at in admiration, for within it, and supported by theology, there has been domination which has deprived many, especially women, of their responsibility. Today in many nominally Christian families there is great reluctance to train children because we have moved so far in reaction to earlier paternal excesses. It is also true that in most of Western Europe and North America we have forgotten how to hold the aged within a family circle. So we need to confess that frequently this context where each person is known and respected as God knows and respects has been damaged by the swings of fashion, and our failures to communicate with each other. I believe that the risen Christ does reach out to us in our family life, for the experience we have of pain-love, freedom-love which we know between partners and between parents and children, is for many the closest we come to the Father, from whom every family on earth takes its name.

There are those in our broken societies of the Western nations whose need of naming has become critical. They are alienated in a dangerous way, not knowing who they are and where they can find wholeness. Some come from a crisis which has destroyed all confidence, some come forward because of medical problems which have upset mental balance, some through grief, some because of shame, some because modern, complex, technical society has submerged them. To meet some of those urgent needs the modern counselling movement has grown up, with its twin parents: Christian pastoral care and psychotherapy. As we have entered just a little way into an understanding of the human mind and the pressures that act upon it, so the technical knowledge has been placed at the disposal of wise counsellors who can help the broken spirit find wholeness again.

There is some suspicion that the counselling movement may replace the spiritual exercises of former generations by techniques which are unsure and without Gospel sanction. Is this, some ask, the new confessional? Is acceptance of my own past the new equivalent for the forgiveness of God? There is obviously a risk here, for when we deal with disturbed and lonely people, our failures to understand them can lead to tragedy. But the possibilities are great. Just as Jesus used the techniques which had authority in his culture (sending the unclean spirit out of a man, for example), so Christians can utilize methods which respect the individual and help the person to 'come to himself'. It is a way of self-knowledge, and that is a way of naming. Self-hate is one of the most corrosive obsessions, for we turn our anger on others who have done nothing whatever to deserve it, and healing begins when we learn to accept ourselves first and others in consequence.

Most pastors have had to deal with the individual who is convinced that forgiveness is impossible. 'I have commiteed the unforgiveable sin and cursed the Holy Ghost, so you can do nothing for me.' There are many variations. For such people the ancient route of penance offers little, and a much deeper exposure of the inner motives is necessary if there is to be healing. So the skills are a ministry to many who have become anonymous to themselves. The key factor of Christian counselling, beyond the technical skill, is the awareness of the presence of God, always the Other who is within every counselling conversation, who welcomes every seeker, who knows the agonies of the heart before we can express them and who brings us, with our burdens, to the point of adoration when we are ourselves before the Lord. Counselling is not the answer to sin, but is a way by which we may be brought to know reality, and ultimate reality is the welcome of Christ. Mary. With all your past, all your striving, all your loving, all your bewilderment, you are Mary whom I have called. Yes, Master. You really are the Lord who called me, and so long as you call me I cannot despair. Those who name us carry forward the ministry of the risen Christ.

5

Peace be Yours

It has become very difficult to restore the word 'peace' to its full, biblical meaning, for the party-slogan, political headline is now so common that we tire of it. Sometimes we seem to batter one another with peace. Much of the propaganda of the super-powers seems dedicated to making peace claims against each other, and this becomes meaningless, like two schoolboys boasting of their great consumption of Mars bars. In the end you believe neither. What the song writers have done for love, the Kremlin and the White House have done for peace. Yet the gift of God remains, and cannot be destroyed by the postures of the great military powers. There is a peace of God which destroys fear, suspicion, alienation and defensive pride, a peace which the world cannot give because the world constantly contributes new strife to replace the old. When Jesus approaches and says 'Peace be yours', he reveals his purpose and his character, and he alerts us again to the fundamental recreation of the world to be at peace with itself and its maker.

Peacemakers are the very children of God. They share God's purpose. But in our world they invariably have a tough task, are frequently misunderstood, are called traitors, have their objectives slandered, and in the end often slip unnoticed into the background. It is a way of the cross.

There are three typical peace-making positions, each being very easily misused and misinterpreted. The first is that of the umpire, the neutral, who stands between the opposing parties and helps them to meet each other and find a middle way that is a possible agreement. Many of the United Nations peace-keeping efforts are of this sort. They recognize that there are valid, or partially valid, claims on both sides, so the line between the camps must be kept secure, without advantage to either side, until there is a broad agreement. In our industrial disputes a referee is often called in because parties have become fixed into incompatible positions. The misunderstanding is that each side tends to see the referee favouring the other; each new suggestion is seen as a giving-way, a partial surrender. So the peace-keeper of this sort is in an unenviable position; compromise is the name of his skill, and compromise, to the embattled parties, whether nations, employers or marriage partners, becomes a dirty word.

But there is another form of peace-making which is vital in our world. Finding a middle way is only a proper route to peace if both parties have a right which has to be preserved. There may not be such a balance. If there is a struggle between light and darkness, good and evil, in our world and our hearts, then a middle way will never recover the peace of God in creation. In that context the peacemaker who is the child of God does not stand in a neutral position, but is wholly committed to one way. This is surely the meaning of those Gospel passages which show us Jesus speaking of conflict. 'You must not think that I have come to bring peace to the earth; I have not come to bring peace, but a sword' (Matthew 10.34). 'It is different now,' he said; 'whoever has a purse had better take it with him, and his pack too; and if he has no sword, let him sell his cloak to buy one' (Luke 22.36).

Here Jesus was speaking of the inevitability of conflict between all that is represented by the Kingdom of God and those forces which would enthrone evil. We cannot be surprised when such occasions arise and when Christians are called to give themselves to one party in a conflict, but we still find it hard to recognize the occasions. Most of us find it easy, with hindsight, to recognize the struggle against Fascism as such a time in world history. Some Christians, of the most conservative variety, see modern Communism presenting a similar challenge, while most black Christians find in apartheid the very face of evil. To be a peacemaker may then mean active struggle, but it took a man from another faith, Mahatma Gandhi, to teach us that the most protracted, crucial political struggle can still be fought without committing violence against others. Since Christians have been warlike in the past, and some still condone war in the present, we need humility to learn how to participate in struggle in a Christ-like way. But struggle there will sometimes have to be if great injustice is to be beaten back. Or else Christian preachers may well find themselves smarting under Jeremiah's accusation.

> For all, high and low, are out for ill-gotten gain; prophets and priests are frauds, every one of them; they dress my people's wound, but skin-deep only, with their saying, 'All is well.' All well? Nothing is well (Jeremiah 8.10–11).

The third peacemaking call comes with the realization that we have damaged the lives of other people and so have contributed to the store of bitterness or injustice in the world. Most of us come to that point at some stage. We tend to get angry or irritable when we have done a wrong to others and cannot find a way to put it right; our guilt is transferred very readily to become accusation of others. But the way of the peacemaker is to recognize the wrong and try to put things back into a right relationship.

> If, when you are bringing your gift to the altar, you suddenly remember that your brother has a grievance against you, leave your gift where it is before the altar. First go and make peace with your brother, and only then come back and offer your gift (Matthew 5.23–24).

The action of peacemaking is given a very high priority, especially when it involves the sacrifice of our self-esteem. Then it becomes the step towards the holy place where we can know the Lord's word. Very few Christian worshippers take this seriously; I suppose we pass it off as a pictorial phrase of the preacher. But it may well be one of the keys to rejuvenate our worship today simply to ask who has something against me and what I can do about it. One of the most puzzling aspects of such peacemaking is trying to put right historic wrongs. Throughout history, injustice has left behind a scar in the mind, even after generations, and sometimes we are challenged to deal with that for the sake of good relationships. Even though we attempt to do this, the earlier injustice is not completely erased; history cannot be wiped from the folk memory, although the Bolsheviks in Russia came close to doing just that, because much of our individuality comes to us from the past. So making amends today for the sins of long ago is a very partial business. We do it in order that living together now in one world may be with mutual respect, and that is a dimension of peace.

In our practical affairs we are often puzzled as to which type of peacemaking we should be involved in. Where one sees a great principle to fight for, another sees a

conflict which must be resolved by finding a middle way.
I have shared in some of the church discussions about the
Falkland Islands and their future, both in Argentina and
in Britain. Both governments profess to see vital princi-
ples at stake. Argentina feels very deeply the need to
obtain sovereignty over territory which she thinks is
properly hers, improperly taken by Britain; this has
become a national rallying-point which unites all parties,
all ages. Britain's official position is that the islands are
rightly hers, by long occupation, and must remain so if
that is what the inhabitants wish. But having talked with
both sides, I am left wondering whether principle is
really the root of the matter, or pride. Britain had no
interest at all before the conflict, so the present posture is
very much that of the victor who holds the prize;
Argentina has no wish to settle in the islands but only to
see the flag flying there, a symbol of ancient wrong put
right. So I believe that some middle way should be
sought. But that is a judgment with which some will
strongly disagree. To take a different example, the
conflict in South Africa seems to me one of those rare
struggles when an evil is being confronted; but there are
others, particularly in Britain and the USA, who see it as
a matter of expediency and practical politics – how can a
white minority maintain a high standard of living amid a
black majority except by ruthless control?

Such examples show how hard it frequently is to
recognize the character of the peacekeeping we are called
to undertake in the world. It is risky to get involved, for
we can always get it wrong, whether it is a political issue
or a marriage that is breaking up. One of the routes we
can take to discover ways to peace is always to look for
the greater unity which lies behind the differences. Since
we are all the people created and loved by God, the final

unity is our place on the globe within God's over-arching purpose and the kingdom of peace where God rules. There is a unity which binds management and shop-floor together; it is the absolute requirement to make an effective industry which can survive but which must only survive with justice to all who work in it. In the dispute which continues in Northern Ireland there are no solutions which an outsider can press on those caught up in such an ancient, emotional struggle. But perhaps there are ways of looking which we can share. There are unities which bind all Irish people, north and south; there is a Celtic history and culture, one of the great treasures of early Christianity; there is a life together in these small islands where our population has intermingled for centuries and cannot now be disentangled; there is a community of Europe in which we all share and where our future political influence will focus. Can we not emphasize the unities?

Those who do, come to us in the closed room, the closed room of our minds or our party or our nationalism or our culture, where we are afraid of exposure, and they say: 'Peace be yours.' Those who speak and live that word come to us with the voice of the risen Christ. That is how we shall experience his resurrection power in our lives and transmit his word of assurance.

6

The Scars of Christ

Somewhere about the year 1225 Francis of Assisi was drawing towards the end of his short life, his body weak with illness and privation but his spirit strong in the confidence of Christ. It is said that during his lengthy solitude and prayer he was overwhelmed with a vision of an angelic figure which lit up the sky above him and wrapped him in the mystery of suffering; and when the vision faded he looked down and saw the marks of the nails in his own hands. Historians are doubtful as to the authenticity of this report, but it certainly comes from sources close to the date. What is sure is the spiritual reality of those scars, for there can have been few disciples of Christ who followed the master so closely, who accepted so large a measure of poverty and ridicule, who worked so tirelessly for the sick and dying, and who radiated so joyful a spirit of life. It was entirely fitting that the physical sign should affirm the inner reality.

But the scars which tell of Jesus Christ are not often so dramatic, nor are all our human scars evangelical. When the heavyweight boxer comes home with a flattened nose no one will recognize in that a witness to the suffering of Christ. What are the qualities which are transparent? The first has to do with the reasons for the suffering. It may be involuntary, something which has been imposed on a person who could not escape or would not evade the challenge. Scars of this sort are carried by people born with a severe handicap of mind or body, inexplicable to those who demand a logical, fair, regular universe, but part of the messy, mysterious process of life in which we are engaged. Others who are marked in this way suffer from childhood in homes that are scenes of battle or utter carelessness or ruthless exploitation. But the most common suffering of this sort is poverty, the kind of poverty from which hard work can never build a way of escape, and which depresses the most enterprising spirit. There may also be scars of voluntary suffering, and here we look for some purpose behind it which has grandness of quality, something more than personal achievement, the giving of self to a great purpose. Some people may regard the soldier's wounds as being in this category, but I think there has to be more than patriotic duty to remind us of Christ; there must be a going beyond duty to faith and love.

Besides the reasons for the suffering we also look at the spirit in which the suffering has been carried. There can be a very unhealthy rejoicing in suffering, a boasting of what we have been through, which is one of the odd faces of human pride. In some groups we even find individuals who feel a need to top others in the suffering scale; the bigger the scars, the more marks! We know others, and perhaps recognize them in ourselves, who receive suffering with bitterness. There is a constant hint of 'It's not fair', or 'I'll get my own back', which may be a sign of toughness of spirit but is also the very stuff of feuds. Such bitterness offers no healing to the world; it keeps the anger alive. In contrast, the scars of Christ are seen in those who have received wholly unjustified blows with a heart at peace, a sense of forgiveness and no clenched fist. We have all been blessed to know such people. I think of them among those with great physical handicaps who yet radiate joy in life. How many blind or deaf or lame people display this quite miraculous absence of bitterness, coupled with joy in living which astounds and encourages us all!

But there is a deeper meaning in the scars of Christ. They testify to defeat. We look back on the experience of the cross in the light of the resurrection and so we see the turning of the parabola, one downward movement balanced by the lifting up to glory. This is the meditation of Paul the apostle (Philippians 2.5–11) and the theme of many hymns. But this can give us a quite unrealistic approach to the cross, removing from it the smell of despair and regret and waste, anaesthetizing the agony. For Jesus in the garden there was no disguising the depth of struggle, and the cry on the cross, 'Why have you forsaken me', affirms the total incarnation. This was no play-acting by one who had the angels in the wings, available for a last-minute rescue. It was deadly serious. For Jesus it was loneliness. The close friends who had followed the way and met the truth could not accept the life which was cut short and the death which was so conclusive. How far away the Kingdom seemed to be as the forces of this world took control and executed their version of justice. The Old Testament is full of images of the pit. The pit or the abyss was the symbol of despair, death, agony of soul, the absence of God (Psalm 28.1; Psalm 30; Psalm 40.2; Psalm 69.15 are examples.) Jesus was there, at the very depth, where the physical pain and the moral loss were combined, and the scars are the marks of that experience.

They are the scars of the risen Christ. The Lord who is always with us is the same Lord who entered into hell. So the cries of suffering in the world meet the response of one who bears that suffering. This sense of kinship has been expressed most vividly in times of war and tragedy as Christians have grappled with the evidence of evil and the promise of salvation. Few have put it with more directness than Studdart Kennedy, during the First World War.

If he could speak, that victim torn and bleeding,
    Caught in His pain and nailed upon the Cross,
Has He to give the comfort souls are needing?
    Could He destroy the bitterness of loss?

Once and for all men say He came and bore it,
    Once and for all set up His throne on high,
Conquered the world and set His standard o'er it,
    Dying that once, that men might never die.

Yet men are dying, dying soul and body,
    Cursing the God who gave to them their birth,
Sick of the world with all its sham and shoddy,
    Sick of the lies that darken all the earth.

Are there no tears in the heart of the Eternal?
    Is there no pain to pierce the heart of God?
Then must He be a fiend of Hell infernal,
    Beating the earth to pieces with His rod.

Then must it mean, not only that Thy sorrow
    Smote Thee that once upon the lonely tree,
But that to-day, to-night, and on the morrow,
    Still it will come, O Gallant God, to Thee.

The Suffering God

The scars mark the reconciling presence of Christ, the intermediary between the world of death and the realm of life, bearing the experience of the abyss in the eternal light and glory of God.

So we recognize the risen Christ in our world today. We know those whose scarred bodies and minds testify to the experience of dereliction – and also to the climb out on the other side. Depression is one of the common features of our society. It has marked many who could not cope with this technical, complex world; who have failed in human relationships and seen friends turn against them; who have seen a precious work destroyed or a child lost; whose hope has been blown out by a burning sense of unworthiness. That is the pit for our generation. I believe that within church life we do not take with sufficient seriousness the large number of those who may put on a front of religion but who inwardly exist in deep darkness. So the appearance of the risen Christ is the pastor, healer, friend who knows that experience from the inside and who has found peace and touched the loving presence of the Lord.

Why is depression now such a common experience? Some would say that it is more readily recognized today but has always been as familiar. They would point to the black moods of many historical characters and the hopeless weariness which was counted in mediaeval days as a sin. Some might quote the verse about Saul:

> And whenever a spirit from God came upon Saul, David would take his harp and play on it, so that Saul found relief; he recovered and the evil spirit left him alone (I Samuel 16.23).

Nevertheless, I believe that this distress has become more common in this generation and that we may be able to trace some of the roots. One is loneliness. A vast number of people in our Western societies are lonely – because old age has separated them from all their friends, because a marriage has broken up, because city life and work can be so anonymous, because we have forgotten how to strengthen the bonds of community. So when blows come, there is no one sufficiently close to be a confidant, and the sorrow turns inward. Another root is our popular and false standards of success. When we estimate ourselves by the current ratings – how much we earn, what sort of car we own and so on – we set up quite unrealistic targets. For every self-made millionaire there are many who fail in their own estimation. And when we start to despise ourselves we soon despise others too. A third root may well be the very speed of change. When education and science, laws and customs, transport and television, buildings and bureaucracy all take on a new face, demanding new responses, then some feel hopelessly inadequate, curl up like a kitten and see no point in living. Among those three areas we find the origins of much depression; this is how we dig the pit.

The salvation which Christ brings is the other side of the pit. He comes with the scars on his hands and feet as one for whom even the sun became dark, and the Father was absent. But as he shows the disciples his hands he shares that most powerful of all hope, a hope based on experience. So the victim of torture in a terrorist camp, the innocent beaten up by the secret police, hidden away, alone, who yet comes among us with serenity, dynamism and truth, is the living Christ for us, leading us from depression to mountain. When we doubt where Christ is today in a torn and frightening world, then we should look among the wounded.

7

The Living Word

The most loved account of the risen Christ is probably that given to us by Luke about the Emmaus Road. It touches us at many points: the evening light, the dusty road, the mystery and yet the homeliness. It is the world or our everyday conversations. 'Don't you know what has been happening in the city this week? Didn't you hear the rumours? Come and have a bite of supper.' But there in the early part of the account we read of Jesus, unrecognized, exlaiming, 'How dull you are! How slow to believe all that the prophets said. Was the Messiah not bound to suffer thus before entering on his glory?' Then he began with Moses and the prophets and explained to them the passages which referred to himself in every part of the scriptures (Luke 24.25–27). It was surely the most astonishing, authoritative Bible study of all time. How we wish there had been a shorthand writer present! Yet that, too, might lead us astray, leading us to think that there is only one dominical way of teaching the scripture. Jesus used scripture in various ways, sometimes pointing to the contrast between himself and scripture (e.g. Matthew 5.43–44; Luke 11.32) and sometimes quoting scripture to affirm his ministry (e.g. Luke 4.18–19; Mark 11.17).

In this case there can be no doubt that Jesus was pointing to passages of scripture which spoke of the deliverer, his sufferings and his victory, passages which had been interpreted in many ways over a long period but which now, at last, were plain. I can only put forward a suggestion that Psalms and Isaiah were outstanding texts in this tutorial. Psalms have so many verses about suffering and deliverance. Isaiah has that rhythm as the very pattern of the book: God's calling, disappointment, sorrow, redemption through suffering, recovery, celebration. But whatever the precise texts, Jesus was applying them to himself. The word written had become the word lived.

This passage reminds us that as Jesus both honoured the scripture and interpreted the words, so those who speak in his name have the same commitment. For us the honouring of scripture goes further because it is only through scripture that we have come to know the character of God and his saving action in Jesus Christ. Jesus could point to veiled hints in the ancient writings; we can point to the life of Christ described by his followers. This is the ground for the authority which we give to scripture, its account of God made known with clarity in person. The authority is God's and only in a secondary way attaches to the book. As God speaks to us through the book, so we know that this is a word to be obeyed. All too often Christians have treated the book in such a pedantic or superstitious way that they have reversed the saving gift; the living word has become the printed word.

A typical way in which this happens is obsession with detail. During my ministry in the South Pacific islands of Polynesia, one of the most popular church events was the *uapou*, a Sunday evening village hymn singing. At the start of the evening a Bible passage was set or questions put, and between each hymn anyone could stand up with comments or questions. The village characters could tell stories and the shy youngsters could display their knowledge, and everyone was relaxed in the glow of a hurricane lamp under the stars. But what often impressed me was that, however splendid the initial Bible reading, the responses tended to become more and more trivial, and often ended up with heated argument about whether a whale could swallow Jonah or who was the wife of Abel. Perhaps this is a sign of our common escapism from the deep personal questions to the peripheral ones which will not disturb our way of life. There can be such attention to the minutiae of scripture that we lose the strong sense of the central message. Jesus on the Emmaus road reminds us that scripture points to him as its fulfilment and hope; when we follow that way we are likely to draw most life from the written page.

But that is a polemical statement. It is placing our statement of faith in front of our reading and then using it as a value judgment, although we only arrive at our faith conviction through the scripture. It can become a neatly circular argument to baffle the unbeliever. Read this to discover faith; have faith and then you will understand what you read. The centre of this circle is, of course, the reality of God who actively discloses himself to his creation. The scriptures testify to that disclosure. The Lord comes in exodus and law, in prophet and priest, in saint and Saviour, but if there is no disclosure to me then I can only study a historical record which takes its place beside other works of ancient history. Whether or not the revealing of God reaches my heart and mind is a mystery. There is no guarantee, no process which ensures a creative result. But the depth of meaning grows with each step of faith; as we commit ourselves to the truth we know, so we can enter into new insight and challenge. I do not share the modern scepticism about biblical scholarship, for I believe it has been an unparalleled tool to uncover the nature of the biblical record, to explain its development over many centuries and to assess the intention of the writers. We are thankful for the patient tasks of scholarship. After such scrutiny we can have great confidence in the text itself.

The interpretation in faith leads us from text to Christ. One of the marks of the renewal of the church in Latin America has been the discovery of the power of scripture when interpreted by ordinary people through their experience. The preaching of Jesus about the Kingdom of God takes on fresh reality when the village is struggling to escape from a reign of terror, for then the questions of the moment are seen as the questions of eternity. What is our life? Can we escape from evil? Who offers real hope and not just political promises? And those involved in crisis have a fresh vision of the infinite struggle between good and evil, cross and resurrection, as though personal risk becomes a lens through which the critical questions become plainer. So study of the text, faith in the reality of God and action to fulfil the prayer of Christ are three partners which bring us as close as we can ever come to the travellers on the Emmaus Road.

Yet the honour we bring to the written text, even from the best of motives, is a risky business. Honour very easily slips into literalism, the tragedy of historical religion. This was the trap for Judaism which led many of its best scholars to become legalists who could 'tithe mint and cummin', the smallest details of religious law, while neglecting justice and mercy. If every sentence of a written text carries equal weight, and each has behind it the authority of the Holy Spirit, then detail becomes as powerful as the whole message of salvation and soon we are lost in a maze of words. This particular risk is enlarged within the Calvinist tradition with its emphasis on the Word of God. When we shift the focus of worship from the sacraments to the sermon, and the focus of church order from tradition to the Bible, then we are readily caught in the intellectual games of those who hunt for texts to support every possible point of view. Some of us need to confess that we fall under that judgment when we review our preaching. What is the weight of scripture as our authority for the life of the church today? Our world is very different from the biblical world, our horizons are much wider, our understanding of the mechanisms of the world much greater, and our vision of human culture much broader. So a mechanical application of scripture might be as inappropriate as taking Mrs Beaton for the guide to modern kitchens, or Machiavelli as the instructor for today's parliamentarians.

We are saved from this risk only if the resurrection has power and meaning for us. The dead Christ and all the history about him would be of the same quality as Plato's *Republic* – fascinating, wise, stimulating – but belonging to an age and a society that is not ours. The living Christ is the interpreter. He makes scripture the food for our hearts as he teaches us on our dusty roads today.

What does that mean? Is that another preacher's gambit? This is exactly where the resurrection is hope for every Christian, for there are no clerical trade unions which have control of scripture. If Christ is alive then the words of an old book are testifying to one reality – the historical revelation – but communicated to our hearts by a living reality. When preaching is powerful we sense this happening. The living Christ is not only known in the text, but also in the interpretation, so that past and present are both subject to the same Lord. We are rightly unwilling to claim too much, and as soon as any Christian claims to be the very voice of Christ we all recoil in dismay. Yet we know it can happen. The Lord of scripture can take the study we do, the prayer we offer, the intelligence we bring and the passion to communicate which overcomes our nerves, and we find the words becoming life and meaning as Jesus was for his friends.

We each have our moments of such revelation. There was a moment for me a long way back in the Pacific islands when we had gathered in Samoa for the first ecumenical conference of the island churches. We came from the established, conservative churches which were often living on the strengths of a previous generation. Their biblical study was very traditional. But in Samoa we had welcomed Hans-Ruedi Weber from the World Council of Churches to lead our Bible study and the text was the Epistle to the Galatians. Both man and text were wise choices. We were confronted once again by the gift of grace and the bonds of law. We saw the danger to the spirit that comes from a legal programme for righteousness. At the end of the conference Hans-Ruedi Weber said: 'Now we will act out the message of Galatians', and he climbed on to the table at the front of the hall and did a mime of the imprisoned spirit throwing off the bondage of the law and entering into the freedom of sonship. The message and the manner of it came as a living word. That was in 1960, and Dr Weber is still stimulating us with the clarity of his insight and the vivid forms of his expression.

Did not our hearts burn within us when we heard that interpretation of the text? The living Christ gives life to the words. This will always be the answer to literalism: that the living Christ leads us now to understand God's will, for he is not trapped in what was written about him. The Christian and the church can make mistakes in interpretation; every possible mistake has surely been made at some point of our Christian history. So patience, prayer and the fellowship are essential to us when we study scripture: patience in the long search for the mystery of God's glory in suffering, prayer that we may walk in the company of Christ, and the fellowship in which personal oddities are corrected and relationships tell of the company on the road.

8

The Breaking of Bread

There can be few simpler actions than breaking bread, but what great complexities have surrounded it through the centuries! The varieties of Christian devotion have led the people of God to place different emphases here. The common meal, sign of community; the sacrifice of Christ made present for us; the feeding by God of his people; our participation in the life and death of Christ; the foretaste of the heavenly banquet; the renewal of our pledge to God; celebration of God's gift to us – all these and more are facets of the one reality. Christians have also varied greatly in the weight they give to this dimension of faith. For the Orthodox and Catholic traditions, the feast or eucharist is so central that nothing approaches it in importance as a form of worship. For the Society of Friends and the Salvation Army it has never been a necessary part of their devotion to Christ. This wide diversity has led to deep conflicts in the past – about meanings, about discipline and order, and about the place of the meal in Christian life. Today our concern is to accept one another, but sadly division and not just diversity remains to judge us.

Here our concern is with only one dimension of the communion. That does not mean that it is the supreme element. It is just the aspect of the meal that testifies to the resurrection faith, and declares in action what the

New Testament declares in words. If the person outside the Christian faith looks in at a service of holy communion, one major impression is likely to be that these people, so strangely venerating a crumb and a sip, must be honouring the memory of their dead leader. They read his words, the observer might report, and think of his death and toast him as those who are for ever indebted to a sacrificing and charismatic teacher. But we would respond that the most vital element has not been seen. Christ is known and is present in the breaking of bread. That was the eye-opener for the Emmaus pair and still has power to bring the living Christ to our consciousness today.

This has been described in various ways through the centuries. One strong tradition has spoken of the priest who breaks the bread standing in the place of Christ, the image or icon given to the church. This view is associated with priestly exclusiveness. Only the priest in a specific tradition can stand and effect the blessing of the sacrament. There have been exaggerated versions of this in the past. A Catholic bishop in Austria in the early years of this century could write to his flock, 'Where in heaven is there such power as that of the Catholic priest? With the angels? With the Mother of God? Mary conceived Christ the Son of God in her womb and bore him in the manger at Bethlehem. Yes. But consider what happens at Mass. Does not the very same thing happen, so to speak, under the consecrating hands of the priest at the moment of transubstantiation? Once did Mary bring the divine child into the world. But lo! the priest does this not once but hundreds and thousands of times as often as he celebrates.'* The priest here becomes the essential key to

*Johannes Katschtaler 1905; quoted by J. S. Whale in *The Protestant Tradition*, CUP 1955.

making Christ real for Christians. The passage also points to the view that the elements of bread and wine are the conveyor of Christ and that the priestly act of consecration is when the Holy Spirit acts to bring Christ to us.

It is impossible to dismiss such testimony which has lived for so long in such a large section of the church. I find that sometimes within the Reformed tradition there can be such carelessness about the elements that one begins to wonder whether we see any real connection between them and the living Christ. That is the worst side of our practice. So there is a welcome for the reverence which, in Catholicism, surrounds the mystery of the sacrament. Even so, I am thankful for all those parts of the church which have left behind priestly dominance and have learned to respect the sacred character of the whole fellowship at the communion. Is the priest an icon of Christ? No more than every Christian who has received the grace of forgiveness. Indeed I am thankful that there are always people in the congregation who are better icons than I am. The early phases of the tradition which locates all the sacramental power in the priest has far more to do with the worship of a thousand Roman temples than with the presence of Christ, the teaching of Christ or the experience of the apostles. Just as there was mutual influence between theology and nationalism at the time of the Reformation, so the religious milieu of the early church affected its orders and its ordering. So while we may maintain a position that certain persons are authorized to preside at the sacrament as part of our understanding of discipline in the fellowship, it is foolish to place here the power to convey Christ's presence with his people.

Does that power lie in the elements themselves? The

long theological arguments about this question have shown the church at its worst, often misrepresenting one another, giving too much weight to words, cherishing separated traditions. Christ is risen. We do not celebrate around a corpse. The risen Christ comes to his people, and one form in which he comes is through the humble, physical elements we eat and drink. Christ surely is known to us in this manner, but not exclusively so. One term in the ancient controversies which has always puzzled me is the 'real presence' of Christ in the eucharist. I do not believe that there is ever an unreal presence. If Christ is with us, then that is really true; it is real, not a figment of the imagination. And if Christ is present then it is the same presence, not graded into first-class presences at the eucharist and third-class in the carol service. Even to speak in such terms is to de-personalize Christ and move into the world of magical effusions.

It seems to me much more satisfactory to think of the presence of Christ in the total action of the meal: in the prayers, the invocation, the breaking and pouring, the distribution, the eating and drinking, the response of commitment, the blessing and the fellowship in which these acts take place. To isolate one factor and make that determinative is unnecessary, since it inevitably down-grades the other factors. The priest or minister who presides surely does witness to the Lord who broke the bread. The bread witnesses to the Lord who was broken. The peace tells of the Lord who reconciles today. The fellowship is the body of Christ, alive with his spirit. I think of the breaking of bread as the signal which enables the eyes to be opened so that we know who has been with us on the road.

It is one of the sorrows of our history that so much

exclusiveness has surrounded the sacrament, fencing it from fellow Christians. We have always offered the most holy reasons for this. We do not want to cheapen the feast, to make it so easy that it can be approached without thought or care. We seek a community of faith at the table, a wide agreement on what we are doing and what God is doing in the service. To match our theological problems we have, in the past, built a physical fence around the holy table in many churches. This has encouraged the thought that only holy people are welcome. So there are some places where a large proportion of worshippers leaves the church when holy communion begins. All these forms of exclusion conceal the resurrection Christ.

It is Christ who welcomes us, and there is a real sense in which the sacrament does not belong to the church but to the church's Lord. If he calls, 'Come to me all who are weary and carry heavy loads', then no fences of ours can stand in the way. To ask for a total unity of faith before we share communion together is equivalent to pushing the experience away to the end of history, for at no time will all Christians be agreed on all Christian doctrine. And to think of the sacrament belonging to the righteous is to turn the Gospel upside down, for it is precisely those aware of sin who are invited to seek forgiveness, while those who are quite oblivious of their sin find no renewal and no food for their souls. Just as Christ on the cross has his arms opened wide to the world, so the risen Christ offers an open-armed welcome to all seekers, pilgrims, children, penitents, handicapped, all who have a long-ing for God and all who give themselves for justice and righteousness in the world. The fences have much more to do with the excessive institutionalism of church life than with the christology of the New Testament.

But most of us have, in one way or another, narrowed down the wonder of the sacrament. We often regard it in very individual terms as an act of private devotion, a dialogue between me and my Lord, so that other people present are a distraction. Such narrowness is encouraged by the common European understanding of faith. We have long ago lost the sense of the people together as the pilgrim people led by the Lord towards the holy city, and we have commonly substituted a private faith-contract in which my devotion and God's forgiveness combine to give assurance of blessedness. I do not see how it is possible to escape from our particular cultural emphasis, and perhaps we can only begin to do so through experience of other cultures. But to realize that this particular narrowing has taken place is some defence against its pietistic excesses. The corporate nature of the meal is a basic element. The company at the table is both those we touch and the far greater congregation beyond our sight, and our personal faith encounter is part of that age-old approach to the mystery of God.

Another narrowing which is common is to isolate the sacrament from the rest of our human life, to make it totally other, to surround it with the most elaborate of liturgy, to speak it in archaic language, to dress it in the most splendid robes and to lift up the chalice of shining gold. There may be moments in our pilgrimage when all this elaboration perfectly fits the spiritual occasion, the high days of celebration. But it is a dangerous diet. If Christ comes to us dressed in such finery, we may romanticize him out of our ordinary lives. Sacrament and daily life belong together, and we need symbols of that, too.

The most strenuous narrowing must surely be that sacramentalism which puts the spotlight of spiritual attention solely on the elements, and allows a biblical literal-

ism there which would be dismissed in general. Many of
us have spoken the words 'This is my body which is for
you', lost in wonder but unsure of the dimension of the
claim. My own background and experience lead me to
think that we cannot rigidly identify the elements,
offered to God, as flesh and blood. When we think of
Jesus at the table saying these words it is very difficult to
imagine the disciples hearing them as 'This bread is now
my flesh.' In John's Gospel the comparable saying is
given in chapter 6.51, where the connection between
bread and flesh is explicit. It is significant that John does
not record this saying as part of the ritual of the Last
Supper – where the attachment of 'flesh' to a specific
piece of bread would be inescapable – and includes it in a
long discourse which leads from ordinary food to spiritual food. The verse is John's climax to the teaching. It
must surely be true that the disciples remembered the
phrase in the light of the supper, and this informed much
later discussion. But it strains our historical sense to
think of the disciples at the table eating bread and
receiving it as the flesh of the one who was there before
their eyes. It makes more sense to me to understand the
words as, 'This breaking of bread is how my body is
broken for you. This is how my death will be known
among you until the end.' Such an interpretation is not
the most common in Christian history, but it belongs to
an awareness that resurrection is our doorway into the
life of Christ. Our concentration is then not so much on
the eating and drinking of the flesh and blood of the
Lord, which can become a crude play-acting, as on the
very life and love of Christ into which we are joined by
grace, and which become our life and our love through
the Holy Spirit.

A powerful plea comes to the churches from the Taizé

community: 'Aim at simplicity.' So little is needed to clothe this action of faith. The commitment of hearts and minds, concentrating on the gift of Christ; the peace between neighbours; bread and wine; deep prayer; the song of praise – and the living Christ is known to us, his self-offering is our blessing, and his victory is assurance for us all.

9

Beach Breakfast

There is a homeliness and informality about the Galilee setting which distances us from fear. The wonder is still there. We read of the miraculous catch of fish. Some commentators, impressed with the naturalness of the context, dispute the adjective. Perhaps, they say, the shadow of the shoal was more easily seen from the beach than from the boat, so Jesus was just offering friendly advice. There is no way of checking the conditions of wind, water and sunlight on that day, no way of disputing any explanation. Rather, we have to draw out of the events the character of Christ which is shown in his relationship to the disciples and to us.

The plainest characteristic is friendship. During the ministry of Jesus we do not have many instances of informal, family-type occasions recorded, because all the interest of the evangelists was in the ministry, the teaching, healing and worship. But there must have been many occasions of that sort. To be itinerant with a small group on the dusty roads, among small towns, resting in olive groves, crossing dried-up river beds, seeking lodging with friendly hosts and with no lecture-room platform, surely implied a continual interplay of companionship among the disciples in which Jesus shared. What we read in the Gospels is only one per cent of the whole history of three years. So we miss the lesser events.

But when we reach the resurrection narratives, each appearance is so crucial that every story is told. It is here, on the lake shore, that we see Jesus befriending the group of still-bewildered men, first by rescuing their vain efforts to bring home a catch of fish and then by offering them a breakfast. The recognition was not immediate, but the scene is very recognizable. The weary, disappointed men in the boat were like ourselves when we have worked hard with little achievement to show. The voice from the shore rescued them from an empty-handed return, just as Jesus had previously rescued them from the storm waves on the same lake. They were familiar waters. Amazed, awe-struck and, no doubt, rejoicing in the abundance, the disciples knew their source of joy and made their way to his presence. Then the invitation to breakfast followed quite naturally: we can picture the driftwood fire, the excited, hungry men and the satisfying smell of grilled fish. The Lord and Master, the eternal Word, Messiah, was now the intimate friend.

Friendship carries with it an element of this history, for there is in friendship an aspect of God's way for the human family. It is not a small thing that Jesus declared the disciples to be friends during the meal in the Upper Room. He was offering a level of intimacy that broke open all the old images of a dominant teacher. We cannot imagine Moses, for example, saying this about the elders of Israel, nor Elijah, but these were the two exemplars who appeared with Jesus in the transfiguration. It was a very personal approach by Jesus and an aspect of the king-dom-life which took form in the presence of Jesus. We thank God for friendship.

It enables empathy, the gift of entering into another's experience, of seeing through another's eyes. We rejoice with those who rejoice and weep with those who weep, wrote Paul in the fellowship of the young church, but this is not something which grows to order, and in many parts of church life it has hardly begun to grow. It is more than saying prayers for the bereaved. It is actually feeling the loss ourselves. The weeping is probably easier than the rejoicing part of this, for the success of another often creates feelings of envy in us. If that church is growing while ours is declining, we do not readily throw our hats in the air and burst out cheering. But friendship develops this sense of identity. With close friends we do not have to explain our moods, for they are already understood, just as Jesus saw the disappointment, frustration and hunger in the disciples. How undervalued friendship has been in Christian theology, as though it is mundane, shallow, of no significance. But the entry of God into the world of intimate human relations is a precious dimension of the incarnation. Jesus was feeling for the leper, the centurion, the blind beggar and the hungry crowd on the hillside. He knew, as it were from inside, the doubts in Thomas and the moodiness of Peter.

So we move beyond the objective prayer for others towards identification. This takes shape for me in the experience of the world church. There is a stage in our Christian life where we regularly pray, for example, for oppressed Christians and for those, in South Africa, who are caught up in a struggle for justice. The prayer is genuine even though we have no personal knowledge of those we pray for. The next stage is when we know ourselves to be hurt as our friends are hurt, so that the church begins to live as a single body. We begin that experience in a local church, where faces and names and homes and needs come together. At the other end of our growth there will be a broader

sense of unity than anything yet known, and to that
end we are committed. We may, by grace, reach the
point where we know the reality of John Donne's
sermon, that 'any man's death diminishes me'. For
many of us the ecumenical fellowship is the context in
which deep friendship has grown, and that is not the
least of its gifts to us. When friendship grows between
the Baptist and the Roman Catholic, the Pentecostal and
the Presbyterian, then the barriers between them cease
to have that edge of prejudice which has embittered
relations in the past.

It is in the context of developing friendship that we
are able to carry through the difficult process, often
claimed but seldom achieved, of 'speaking the truth in
love'. Very often this phrase from Paul's letter to the
Ephesians has been used in the church as a cover for
cattiness, petty cruelty or envy when the critical spirit
overwhelms our reticence. It is even used as a defence
when we criticize a colleague behind his or her back. 'Of
course, I don't want to criticize, but we have to speak
the truth in love and my minister completely failed . . .'
That was the very opposite of Paul's meaning when he
wrote the phrase. He was writing about growth into
'mature manhood, measured by nothing less than the
full stature of Christ' (Ephesians 4.13). In that process,
he urged, we grow best when we share the truth of
Christ within a loving fellowship. That is the context
where our hearts, minds and wills are shaped together.
No longer are we in the classroom, hearing what is sent
down to us and forgetting most of it the next day or next
year, nor are we in the courtroom hearing accusations,
nor in the market-place hearing the advertiser's boast,
but we are among friends who will still be beside us
even if we disagree. There is thus a very close connec-

tion between friendship and fellowship – one so often
considered secular and the other sacred. Both have a
quality of Christ-likeness and both announce the victory
of unity over separation.

Friendship enables us to ask for help without feeling
inferior, and to welcome guests without fuss. But at
its deepest it enables sacrifice to be offered and
acknowledged without glory or shame, as a quite
proper gift to be shared. In friendship a well-paid job
can be given up, a dream holiday forgotten, prized
privacy surrendered, a chance to excel ignored and
even life laid down. When such sacrifice is given out of
duty only, there is often resentment surrounding it (I
slaved for years . . .), but friendship sets it free. It is
not a coincidence that Jesus called the disciples his
friends on the very night when one of them went out
into the darkness to betray him. He was sealing the
relationship in every way he could, deepening it,
affirming it, and in that context it could be said that he
would go out to die.

The text in John 15.15 points to another facet of
friendship – no secrets. There was not one lofty standard
of knowledge from which small titbits were offered to
plebeian minds, but a total sharing of all that was in the
heart of Jesus. We find this rather hard to believe. It is
somehow more comfortable to think that Jesus had
access to a vast computer-bank of knowledge of which
we see only the outer edges. But he hid nothing. That is
not to say that the disciples understood or remembered
everything. Any limitation was on their side, not with
Jesus. This aspect of friendship is a great joy and rarely
found in adults who usually have secrets to keep. It is
very much part of the passionate friendship of children
which we often wish we could recapture. When we do

find such mutual confidence it is a treasure which brings close to us the quality of Jesus.

But the friendship of Jesus, at that point in the narrative, was close to the end of his physical presence with the disciples. There is a non-clinging character about him. One of the less attractive faces of friendship is when it binds us, ties us down, never leaves us alone. Possessiveness is a negative aspect of love. Jesus was preparing to give to the half-understanding disciples, so unsure of their place in Israel and their future in the world, complete charge of the gospel treasure. How could they handle the great mystery of the kingdom which was present in the king, and how might they misinterpret the sayings of their teacher? Jesus trusted his friends. This seems to me an aspect of friendship which brings us close to Jesus himself. It means a full acceptance of what the friend is and does, without jealousy or fear. This is still how Jesus treats us in spite of the very uncertain qualities we demonstrate every day. And this is how he comes towards us in the depth of friendship.

Come along, lads, let's have breakfast. What a blessing that we have not surrounded this event with liturgy and ceremony, but have allowed it to remain an informal incident in which confidence was built up then and is built up now. The one who spoke like that is one of us. But when the meal was over there was to be a very serious conversation, just as after the supper there was a cup of wine. The informality blends into, and enables the dialogue to move towards, the deep things of faith. How often this is true to our experience. Some of the most moving worship we know is in the context of conferences where we have had the most lively social life, the most free and easy relationships, conversations and games, and out of that we turn without any difficulty to the challenge of the word of God that reaches into the secrets of our hearts. This is part of the rhythm of our emotional life, too often neglected by religious people. Come along, lads, what about a barbecue on the beach?

10

Global Commission

In all four Gospels the last appearance of the risen Christ is accompanied by a word of commission or command. The traditions which are preserved by the evangelists have very different features, but that same quality of authority at their centre. The tradition preserved by Luke comes to us at the beginning of Acts, and that in Mark is not found in all the manuscripts, so some consider it a later addition.

Matthew 28.18–20

Full authority in heaven and on earth has been committed to me. Go forth therefore and make all nations my disciples; baptize men everywhere in the name of the Father and the Son and the Holy Spirit, and teach them to observe all that I have commanded you. And be assured, I am with you always, to the end of time.

Acts 1.8

But you will receive power when the Holy Spirit comes upon you; and you will bear witness for me in Jerusalem, and all over Judaea and Samaria, and away to the ends of the earth.

Mark 16.15–16

Go forth to every part of the world and proclaim the good news to the whole creation. Those who believe it and receive baptism will find salvation; those who do not believe will be condemned.

John 21

Feed my lambs. Tend my sheep. Feed my sheep. Follow me.

There is a clear distinction between John and the other three. John records a word addressed personally to Peter, following the beach breakfast, which balances the previous denial by Peter in Jerusalem. It is interesting that Mark, who based his narrative on the preaching of Peter, does not have this record and some scholars have suggested that perhaps Mark's original ending to his Gospel was lost. But John was reflecting on a most intimate memory and the surprise there is that he does not record a commission to the group as a whole. It may be that the whole weight of Christ's calling to the Twelve is given by John in the conversation in the Upper Room, just as he provides the words of the institution of the Last Supper much earlier in the Gospel. So the evangelist makes what is particular of much wider reference, and makes personal what might become vague.

There is a tremendous geographical note in these sayings, an eye on the world map which must have astonished people with an entirely local history. All nations, the whole creation and the ends of the earth – the commission could not be broader. All those who heard it, in tiny minority groups with no organization, caught up in the Spirit but with the minimum of learning, frequently composed of the 'lower orders' and faced with the supreme military organization of Rome, must have been baffled by the grandeur of the Lord's vision. Then there is a personal note. My disciples, witness for me, follow me. It is the personal witness that is to be the central element of the message, not any philosophy or religious scheme of things. Third, there is an objective: proclaim, bear witness, make disciples. The commission of Jesus has at its heart a longing that all may hear how the kingdom has come to the earth in the person of the king and that all may live in the kingdom-way. It is not a word prophesying great success, and carries no hint of imperial triumphs to come. But the hope of universality is here at the very birth of the church. Fourth, there is a note of authority. The one who speaks has a right to speak. In all the narratives the words come as commands, not good advice and not questions for discussion.

Can we still recognize this voice of authority in an age when 'doing your own thing' is one of the marks of freedom? Authoritarian figures and structures are highly suspect, and for good reason. We have seen too much totalitarian power, too much trampling on the powerless to be at home with a dictatorial gospel or church. There is a key distinction here. The authority of Christ to call us and send us has no army to enforce it and the ordinary person can simply reject it. The authority carries authority when we recognize who speaks. This is the story of the ministry of Christ in the Gospels, that many people could not or would not recognize any authority in him, for he did not live as one of the priestly or princely families. Those who first answered the command 'Follow me' were wholly remarkable in seeing before them an extraordinary man whom they should obey. It was during the ministry that their first response was confirmed. Even the winds and the waves obey him. Never man spoke like this man. 'To show you that I have authority to forgive sins, get up, take your bed and walk.' 'You call me Master and Lord, and rightly, for so I am.' 'You would have no power at all over me unless it had been given you by my Father.' So the words multiply, and the Gospel writers affirm quite plainly that there was in Jesus the authority which is Godly, which belongs to God. That is the recognition which calls us to obedience to this man.

Is it possible to recognize such authority today, and to hear such a word of command? Who can speak such a word? In the tradition of the Reformed churches we have rejected the supreme authority of a pope to represent that authority of God. Yet we have never fully come to terms with the consequences. When the Reformation put the Word of God as the supreme authority but could not define any single route to its interpretation, and when the Reformers themselves differed quite seriously about the meaning of texts, the weight of authority tended to become individual choice. Of course there were balances. There were calls to listen to the preachers who had studied the Word. There was a very clear plea to listen to the fellowship when there was a corporate or conciliar decision. But I believe there remained and still remains an ambiguity. At its best our sense of authority enables us to seek together a conscientious view of what the Lord would have us do. Sometimes we reach that point and know within ourselves that a course of action is right. At its worst we are at the disposal of individual whim, or of an assembly swayed by the rhetoric of one person who may be in error. Then the authority assumed can lead us far from God.

I do not see any guaranteed way of transmitting the authority of Christ to the succession of disciples through history. Popes, we know, can err, and so can bishops and church councils. I know that my judgment can be off-course, affected by mixed motives, ignorance or inattention. So perhaps the error is to look for a guarantee at all. In matters of faith where we seek to know the mind of God in the complex realities of our day, we walk by faith and not by guarantees. I believe this to be specially important when we face new problems where old directives no longer apply, as, for example, in modern medicine or in atomic energy. A claim to issue an authoritative Christian word on such matters is suspect, and we are wiser to take a slower route of discovery. A questioning mind is not disloyalty to Christ, but I suspect that a mind which accepts blindly what is said only because it comes from a priest or a council may be – for then we may actually silence conscience and placidly surrender to the *status quo*. Jesus did not behave in a way which gave comfort to the authorities, and there have been times when church people have needed a similar questioning spirit. So without guarantees we seek the authority of Christ which is never more than partially transmitted to us by the authority of the church.

The clearest sign of authority, as with Jesus, is the nature of the speaker. When a word is spoken to us by one who has been through a great trial, and has come through without bitterness, with forgiveness and hope, then the words spoken carry special weight. When we are called to serve by one who has given a life of service, we recognize authority. The person authenticates the message. It is not like the army, where the rank carries authority regardless of the quality of the individual, for we are considering a moral and spiritual authority. So with us it is the saints of God – those who are transparent to the Holy Spirit – who call us and send us.

But there is another aspect of the commission of Christ. The disciples went out with great confidence into an often hostile world because they had been sent. It was not just a bright idea that they should travel the Roman roads, an inclination of the moment. They were given strength by Jesus Christ in the very act of commission. I can testify to the reality of this in my own commissioning as a young ordinand. I was in no doubt that I should respond to the call for help that came from churches overseas, and so offered for missionary service. But my own inclination was to go to East Asia, and that is the preference that I expressed to the missionary society. In the event I was sent to the islands of the South Pacific, to a place we could not even find in the atlas at home. The only way to reach such a destination was to be sent. And it did give a very strong sense of confidence that this was the place to be. I had not chosen it, had not fallen in love with it, and could not easily leave it, so it was not dependent on my own fancy. Those who had been there and who had carefully assessed the need thought I could serve them, and so it turned out. I was glad that I was sent.

In our church life today I think it would not be wrong to expect a little of that note of being commissioned. It could never take over altogether, because then we may put far too much power into too few hands. But when there is uncertainty in our minds about the work to do next, or when a piece of work has to be done which attracts no applicants, then there may be room for the church to put its hand on my shoulder and say, 'This is for you.'

In all these New Testament words, right at the end of his physical presence in the world, Jesus speaks a word of command to act for others. This is one of the most distinctive features of the authority of Jesus. There have been other forms of authority in history which have emphasized the self. Do this, accept this discipline and you will become king; go and do battle and you will be victorious, and laurels will be yours. The leader can so pass on his authority as to affirm our inner desire for achievement or fame or success. But in Christ there is still, right at the end, this other dimension: that the going and witnessing are entirely for the sake of others who have had no opportunity to meet Christ in the flesh. This word still stands, although we have to be aware of the different world circumstances in which we hear it. The disciple is still to become an apostle, sent by the Lord. Today we do not face a blank world map, and the geographical element in the calling is of less significance, for there is a Christian community in almost every nation on earth. The ends of the earth, in the Acts phrase, are not a periphery with our country as the hub. Rather, they are those places, communities, sectors, streets, industries where people have not been shown the beauty and healing power and ultimate challenge which are in Christ. They may be next door or across the world. These people have a human right (which is a God-given right) to make up their own minds about the news of God in Christ, and they may totally reject what they hear. We have no authority whatever over that decision in others. That is the humility of the Gospel. But the commission is to present the faith in a form which others can recognize as authentic, reliable and touching their deepest needs.

So the Lord looks to the whole world and to that little company of hesitant disciples, so nervous of the future, and he leaves them with the call to a life of service. It must have been wholly baffling to them. We look back over the centuries and read the words with all the history of the apostolic age in our minds. When first heard, though, the command must surely have sounded beyond comprehension. Can there be rescue for our world, so dedicated to wealth and violence, so deeply divided, so divorced from the way of forgiveness? And is it conceivable that ordinary Christians have a part in the divine calling? Those who can see this calling with clarity and share it with vision and hope still speak to us with the authority of the risen Lord.

11

Interlude

I am waiting at Victoria Station for an old friend to arrive; there is a crowd pressing towards the ticket barrier. No sign. Then a movement, a shape down there along the platform and suddenly I know, he's arrived. No need to see the whole person in close up, for the glimpse is enough.

That tune, that orchestration – why, it bears the signature of Elgar. There can't be any doubt. You just know it is his work.

Yes, I saw that steeply pitched red tile roof, those tall brick chimneys and the dormer windows; I spotted the terraced garden, and I knew – Lutyens must have designed it.

See his eyes, the way he smiles – you'd know whose baby that is without being told.

So you see, members of the jury, that act of violence bears all the marks of the accused. It is as though his personality puts fingerprints all over the crime. He may say he was not there, but the action tells us he was.

* * *

In such ways we recognize, and although we do not see everything, a lively connection is made. Something of that experience lies behind the gospel passages about the resurrection. But in the Gospels it is Jesus who does the offering, takes the initiative, makes the first move. So perhaps other examples provide a clue.

* * *

Suddenly, as I wandered down the market, I heard a shout. 'Bernard!' I was so startled I nearly dropped the eggs. I looked back to see who it was. You could have knocked me down with a feather for it was old Ron. I thought he was in Australia.

Dot, dot, dot, dash. Dot, dot, dot, dash. That's it, it must be, the news coming from London. Quiet. Write it down. The guards will be round in a few minutes.

Now listen carefully, members of the panel, to the mystery guest. Just a few words and then you must tell me who it is.

* * *

Every time there is such a declaration, we are being asked to link the present to the past. Sight and hearing are joined to memory. The gift of today, the new event, is constructed on the foundation of past experience. So our Christian awareness of Christ alive and among us is always related to our understanding of Christ in the New Testament. We do not know God in a vacuum. We know him through his words and actions given to us in the historical record, so the Gospels always remain for us the text which verifies our perception of Christ. He is the same Christ, yesterday, today and for ever, and therefore we have confidence that as he was then so he is now, still speaking the word of peace and breaking the bread.

Of course, the particular ways of recognition in the

resurrection narratives are illustrations and not a limit on the living Christ. They show us characteristic ways in which the Lord is the servant and continues his healing work for the sake of the broken world. There are many other forms in which he comes. The whole world, wrote John, could not contain the books needed to hold every detail of the life of Christ. What was true then must be true for succeeding generations, that there is an extraordinary range of action, word, look, touch, giving, feeding, challenging, loving and dying which bring Jesus into our presence. Alertness to recognize him in our world is one of the marks of discipleship. Every day we expect to meet Christ. For us the world is not a desert, and faith is not just a memory of distant people in dusty places. Christ is alive and each step of our personal pilgrimage is enlivened as we recognize his approach to us.

The test of the resurrection is not to say who moved the stone, nor to describe the biological process, nor to explain what happened to the guards, nor to count the angels, nor to fit events into our theologies, but to ask whether the same Jesus, known in the flesh, was known again and is known today in living power. The testimony that this is true has been the mark of apostolic faith from the beginning. It is still the essential clue to a faithful church.

> Christ is alive! Let Christians sing,
>   His cross stands empty to the sky.
> Let streets and homes with praises ring.
>   His love in death shall never die.
>
> Christ is alive! No longer bound
>   to distant years in Palestine
> he comes to claim the here and now
>   and conquer every place and time.

Not throned above, remotely high,
    untouched, unmoved by human pains
but daily, in the midst of life,
    our Saviour with the Father reigns.

In every insult, rift and war
    where colour, scorn or wealth divide
he suffers still, yet loves the more,
    and lives, though ever crucified.

Christ is alive! His Spirit burns
    through this and every future age,
till all creation lives and learns
    his joy, his justice, love and praise.

Brian Wren, from *Faith Looking
Forward*, OUP 1983

One of the great phrases in our Christmas carols comes from Charles Wesley: 'Veiled in flesh the Godhead see'. It has an important ambiguity about it. Clothed in flesh the Godhead becomes visible. But veils also hide. Hidden away within this strange clothing of flesh, seek the holiness of the Lord God. There was nothing obvious to the world to mark this man from all others; only the inner qualities recognized by the minority and the public signs which, so to say, burst through the ordinary veil of flesh. If we dare to think of what this meant for God, then the incarnation was as much a hiding as a revealing. In that little corner of the empire, in quite insignificant towns and villages, with no ready-made platform, through a humble life and a shameful death, God holds back his ultimate, unimaginable power of creation and judgment. He shows his nature. He hides his eternity. He reveals his longing for mercy and justice and forgiveness. He hides his universal presence with all ages and races and languages. The resurrection and what follows from it see the coming together of the hiddenness and the revealed word. The veil begins to lift and we glimpse through the flesh the glory of God. It is too much for our eyes and so 'he was lifted up and a cloud removed him from their sight' (Acts 1.9).

There is a semi-private quality about the resurrection appearances of Jesus. The days of the crowds, the public preaching and healing, the confrontation with the temple authorities are over. Each meeting with the disciples is relatively enclosed, and no strangers are involved. A reason for this may be the same facing of temptation that is recorded at the beginning of the Gospels when the way of stunning miracles was rejected. To appear walking and teaching in the temple three days after his crucifixion would have been for Jesus much the same as throwing himself off a pinnacle of the temple and walking away unscathed. It would have gathered the crowds in awe and wonder; they would have lauded the wonder-worker; they would have expected ever greater signs of supernatural power; but it would not have established that loving trust in God and that spirit of humility which was the road to the Kingdom. So the intimate occasions are recorded. It was the faith of the few that was to be decisive, and their deepest need was met by the presence of the one whose hands were scarred. This was a fulfilment of 'two or three gathered in my name, there am I, among them'.

> Come, living God, when least expected,
>   when minds are dull and hearts are cold,
> through sharpening word and warm affection
>   revealing truths as yet untold.

Break from the tomb in which we hide you
 to speak again in startling ways;
break through the words in which we bind you
 to resurrect our lifeless praise.

Come now, as once you came to Moses
 within the bush alive with flame,
or to Elijah on the mountain,
 by silence pressing home your claim.

So, let our minds be sharp to read you
 in sight or sound or printed page,
and let us greet you in our neighbours,
 in flaming youth or quiet age.

Then, from our gloom, your Son still rising
 will thaw the frozen heart of pride
and flash upon us through the shadows
 to spread his resurrection wide.

And we will share his radiant brightness
 and, blazing through the dread of night,
illuminate by love and reason,
 for those in darkness, faith's delight.

Alan Gaunt, © John Paul The
Preacher's Press

12

Risen Christ and Holy Spirit

Although Paul found Christians at Ephesus who had not even heard of the Holy Spirit (Acts 19.2), perhaps in our day the position is almost the reverse, for we have all heard a great deal about the Spirit through the development of charismatic movements in all the churches. Yet for most of us this hardly means that we have fully become trinitarian in belief. Rather, it is our style to keep the pieces of belief in separate boxes without thinking of the interplay between them. So there are many today who emphasize the doctrine of creation, the stewardship of the natural world, the finite gift, the beginnings of human freedom and the hope of evolution towards a kingdom-state, without the radical critique required by the doctrine of redemption. And there are others who emphasize the salvation offered by Christ to me, the eternal life which I can enter and the transforming gifts of the Spirit in my life without any sense of the community of God's people through history and the sacramental life. In the same way we may think of the risen Christ and of the Holy Spirit in two compartments. The first occupies us for six weeks from Easter. Then we start thinking of Pentecost. But in every trinitarian theology we must hold the two together.

This is not easy to do. Often we think of Jesus solely in terms of the life in Palestine, that limited period of years. The Spirit may then seem like the invisible replacement of

Jesus, a vague presence by which God assures us of his continuing love. But Jesus and the Spirit are God, eternal as God is eternal. The life of Jesus from Bethlehem to Calvary is part of a continuous being. 'Before Abraham was, I am,' and, 'I am with you always, even to the end of the age'; these are markers of the divine life of Christ. Similarly, many signs of the Holy Spirit are mentioned in scripture before Pentecost, though that event does seem to have been a special, one-off, God-given experience to set the disciples on the new road of public witness. Jesus himself promised that coming. In chapters 14, 15 and 16 of John's Gospel we have the plainest teaching, and when we remember that the Gospel was probably written at the end of the first century, we may see through the narrative to the discussion in the early church about the Holy Spirit. Who, or what, is the Spirit? Why did and does the Spirit come? Such questions have always been raised by Christians.

Very briefly we can note that the Holy Spirit is from God (14.16,25); is sent into human life as helper, companion, counsellor; reveals truth about Jesus (14.26) and about the Father (15.26); leads into all truth (16.13); brings a judgment about ourselves and our relation to God (16.8); and comes in fullness when the visible life of Jesus is over (14.25; 16.7). The whole trend of these chapters is a preparation for the ending of the disclosure of God in the physical Jesus and the beginning of a new relationship in and through the Holy Spirit. There is one movement of salvation, one rescuing God, one recreating power. But history is a line and so God, acting in history, has a history. God in Christ comes at a date in the calendar.

How, then, are we to understand this gift of the Spirit in relation to the risen and ascended Christ? I do not think it of first importance to make an absolute intellectual distinction. Rather, we are concerned with Christian experience. How do we know God and how does he hold us and shape us through a life of discipleship? I want to point towards two responses.

First, there is in the Gospel references to the Spirit a plain indication that God comes to us in the Spirit to teach us the truth, and so to enable us to know Jesus Christ. Here we remember that the apostolic church was not bound, as many of us are, by a tradition of academic scholarship. It was not tied to books. Indeed the formation of the canon of the New Testament took place well after the lives of the apostles, and at first the news of Jesus was passed in sermons and conversation and repeated sayings treasured in the heart. So while we may think that 'knowing Jesus' is the same thing as knowing the scripture, that cannot have been the first meaning.

It is much more to do with forming understanding and judgment. The early Christian period was a time of many religious claimants when voices called to worship in a host of temples and shrines. All over the Middle East the ancient hill-top sanctuaries still had their guardians, while the temples of the Greek and Roman gods graced most large cities and the lesser cults drew those seeking a new knowledge. So it was very easy to be confused. Where is Christ? Can we find him in the tracks of Delphi? Is he a child of Apollo? Are the priests of Ephesus a way to find him? Look, here he is; there he is. And amongst such confusion the Holy Spirit is the inner guide for every seeker, so that in the presence of Christ men and women may recognize him and see God's life made plain. This does not mean infallibility, for the recognition is by men and women who do not receive omniscience. The Holy Spirit, wrote John, will lead or guide you into all truth, not that all truth will be presented on a plate for the taking.

So it is the leading towards truth that is the gift of the Spirit within the human mind, and therefore we treasure the sense of movement, seeking, pilgrimage and readiness to confess ignorance which are marks of the greatest Christian scholars. We all stand in need of this gift. We want to recognize the truth of Christ in the world. We long to see God's grace before our eyes, and make no mistake. But the complexities of religious presentation today may baffle us. If in Ireland some people declare that a statue of Mary has moved, is the Lord at work in it? If an American evangelist builds a glass temple fitted with television cameras, is the Lord there? When a cathedral is lit up with a series of colourful processions, the very best of copes and mitres, is the man on a donkey there too? And when two devoted Christians are on opposite sides of a passionate argument, do I have to see Christ on one side and not on the other? We all need the one who will keep on guiding us all our lives into the truth of Christ.

I do not see gullibility as a Christian grace, for an element of scepticism prevents us from adopting a superstitious variant of Christianity, and many of those have imprisoned the human heart through the centuries. But Jesus reminded his followers of the need for an open, childlike heart. So when confronted with those two arguing Christians we do not fall into the trap of attaching Christ to one side only, but we are likely to respond: 'Both of you are still learning and neither of you has fully arrived.' For example, one of the larger areas of dispute among Christians today lies in our relationship to political systems. Many Christians in socialist countries have become convinced that the way of Christ, the way of fairness to all, is best translated into politics by a socialist system. Others, and most Christians in North

America and Western Europe, regard the capitalist system as better representing the freedom of individual choice which God gave in creation. To claim Christ for one side or the other is very risky, even dangerous, for once we have tied a political/economic system to the Saviour of the world, then the eternal Word is enclosed in a temporary box of human manufacture, and the box is given divine sanction. It is the divine right of kings in new clothes. Far better for us to look beyond both systems if we would see the kingdom of God, to recognize some virtues and some failures in both ways of government, and to know our own preference, to argue for it, but never to hold to it as essential to the Gospel.

How much harder, then, to seek and find truth when we are divided on matters which many regard as essential to the Gospel. There is such a division about the papacy. For some it is an integral part of the gift of Christ through which his will is made known in the church, but for others it is a mistaken continuance of mediaeval leadership in the church. Is this not a dispute in which one must be right and one wrong? I do not believe that would be an adequate response, for our obedience to Christ is not so simply delivered. That a large part of the Christian community has found in the papacy an adequate focus of unity and teaching authority is a fact that has to be recognized by those of us who belong to other traditions. But we also hold to a fact, that many Christians have sought and found a community life of discipleship and a way of understanding the will of Christ which do not depend at all on that one personal leader. Perhaps neither should claim finality for the position we have reached, for then the way forward is more open. Catholics would render a great service to Christian unity by a public recognition that the papacy can be and should be open to renewal and change, for the Holy Spirit still teaches truth about our common life in Christ. Protestants, too, would be true to the fathers of the Reformation if they were ready for change in their understanding of the symbols of unity that are needed in the world-wide Christian family. If there were such openness then at least a possibility of development would exist and there need be no trench warfare.

Those two examples are only illustrations of what it might mean if we take the gift of the Holy Spirit seriously as leading us into truth. It is surely a denial of the Spirit's power if we regard spiritual truth as a wrapped parcel, a Chubb safe of which the professionals have the key. But the pilgrimage is never an easy one; conviction and doubt are both companions on the way; assurance is in the direction of movement and not in the glory of having arrived. The Spirit leads us to Christ.

The second way in which to understand the relationship of the Christian with the risen Christ and the Spirit is the formation and development of Christian character. To me this seems a neglected area in modern theological work, but a very familiar one in previous centuries. The great classical text is in Philippians 3.10–14:

> All I care for is to know Christ, to experience the power of his resurrection, and to share his sufferings, in growing conformity with his death, if only I may finally arrive at the resurrection from the dead. It is not to be thought that I have already achieved all this. I have not yet reached perfection, but I press on, hoping to take hold of that for which Christ once took hold of me. My friends, I do not reckon myself to have got hold of it yet. All I can say is this: forgetting what is behind me, and reaching out for what lies ahead, I

press towards the goal to win the prize which is God's
call to the life above, in Christ Jesus.

Christlikeness does not come to us ready-made. At
whatever age we enter into Christian faith, we know
that the whole of our lives will be needed to take even
the first steps towards that pattern of living and self-
giving and trusting which we see in Christ. We all can
testify to this. It does not require a preacher to tell us
so. It is a long process because we are such a mixture
of ambitions and hopes and appetites and ideals, and
because we cannot avoid hearing the multitude of
voices that cry to us through every channel of human
communication. Sometimes we may think that the
ancient fathers had it easy, in those pre-rat-race days,
when meditation could be given all the time in the
world. But I do not believe anyone has it easy. The
testimony of the saints is that we are always in danger
of moving outside the Christian way and that the
magnetic pull to do so cannot be avoided by monastic
duties. The human character does not easily take the
form of one who gave himself away, for we are in-
clined to be gatherers, graspers, claiming for ourselves
powers or certainties or space or satisfaction which we
deny to others. This was the experience of Paul, the
apostle whose honesty about his own development
shines through the letters even when the precise theological emphasis seems strange to our minds. We
know a man with a complex nature, sensing his battle
of the mind to grasp the dimensions of salvation in
Christ and his temptation to condemn all who did not
see Christ in his way. The constant reaching forward,
the forgetting what is behind, the pressing towards the
goal – all that is a vivid story of the Holy Spirit at work

to change the Paul of Pharisaic legalism into the imitation of Christ.

We are on such a journey. For many of us the main elements of our own religious awareness and conviction were settled during our teens or early twenties. That was the period when other people greatly influenced us and when our character was open to new experience, new patterns. It was when the devotion of the heart was given readily. It was when enthusiasm could conquer caution. Such is the way of growing up and it is surely part of the divine gift of life itself that we have such an opportunity to pledge ourselves to the highest. That still remains the pattern of religious history for many people. The sorrow is that we then stay there for ever. We may attend faithfully at worship for the rest of our lives but remain fixed in the attitudes of those early years of faith. How many of us adopt a resolutely nostalgic approach to church life, wondering where the golden days have gone, and contact with the religious books which fed us then.

The response which the Holy Spirit enables within us is the steady learning of the way. Christians through the centuries have developed varied patterns of devotion and discipline through which they can continuously seek growth into Christ. Within all of us there is a large place for prayer. Failure to grow spiritually very often is caused by failure to pray. God does not force us to pray. The Holy Spirit is not an injection of a spiritual tonic. We can turn aside from the way of prayer on any day of our lives and there will be no lightning strike; we can remain in church membership and we can still act as ministers of the church. But the energy of our pilgrimage will drain away and we will not learn so readily to put on the new being in Christ. All the influence of our secular society is against the regular practice of prayer. Family prayers are now uncommon among church people. No reform of our church life would be as far-reaching as an acceptance of the discipline of prayer in which we deliberately give time to study of the way of Christ and offer to God the way of the world, and so come to see the fusion of the two, the redemption crossing-point in personal and public life. That would surely be the activity of the Spirit to change the Christian community.

The junction of scripture and the contemporary context of our lives is important in another way. The death of spiritual formation comes when we divorce word and action. When we speak the great words and still do absolutely nothing about them, then the dynamic of faith drains away. We are left with the poetry, the images, the rituals, the order but have seen no translation into the world of work and politics and family. That is one of the great tragedies of European Christianity. Our words are splendid, our actions petty. To make the connection is the gift of the Holy Spirit. That was the astonishing experience of Peter at Joppa when he discovered that Gentiles were no longer to be regarded as unclean but could now be part of the one family of grace. So attitude to neighbour was a consequence of trust in Christ. Our Christian formation requires that sort of concrete expression of faith, a new friendship, a fresh struggle for justice, an experience of healing, an outpouring of creativity, which God longs to give to his people.

In such ways the Holy Spirit works in people in order that the very ordinary disciples may become like Christ. Christ lives. We see his face and his hands in the lives of those who have consciously attended to his way of the cross, and in whom the Holy Spirit has given a longing for truth and a wisdom in judgment. God among us, God within us, one God with one purpose to recreate the community of hope and trust in which we are at one with him.

13

Risen Christ and his Body, the Church

The image of the body comes instantly to our minds when we think of the relation of the church to Christ. It is a familiar thought that God, who came among us in the physical body of Christ, now works in the world through the body over which Christ is the head. It is only one of many images, and we need to balance its meaning with others, especially the vine with its branches and the house with its foundation stone. But for our purpose of studying the resurrection, it is certainly a key under-standing of what Christ is doing in the world. Four aspects are obedience, expression, movement and unity.

'He is the head of the body, the church' (Colossians 1.18) is a statement in the present tense. So it is very different from the concept of a school of thought indebt-ed to its founder and seeking to carry out his programme. The martyrs and the gurus, the philosophers and the preachers may all win their followers who will, in a sense, become the physical continuation of the leader in later years. But they all have a fixed, limited body of teaching which cannot be in any way extended. Are Christians in a different position? The tragedy is that for some the position is really no different. Christ is gone into the past and his words are a textbook which has to be learnt. But when we live in the assurance of the resurrection, then we live with a living Lord whose authority is not limited to the events of his physical life. The church has constantly to face new events and challenges which are far removed from the context of the Gospel writers, and there are no solutions to be found simply by quoting the texts. Obedience certainly means knowing the texts. We can never evade the basic Christian duty of that study. There is more to obedience than that, and it is in that next step that the church has so often failed.

During the last two centuries we have come to know both the dimensions of the human family and the extent of human dominance over the natural world. Both these enormous developments have presented us with fresh opportunities to be the body obedient to the head. They have called us to hear the living Christ in this new context. The discovery of the diversity and unity of the human family, the range of human history, the depth of human cultures, the extent of human needs and hungers, the wealth of human creativity and the awesome total of human cruelty and human love – all this has been a moment when the Lord has been speaking to us about the meaning of our humanity and the saving of humanity. We have been given the first chance in history to act out the meaning of 'Our Father . . .' to the full. We know to whom we owe our sisters and brothers across the globe, that they are all of ultimate value to God. But sadly we have been very slow in obedience to this vision. The evidence of this is the narrow nationalism which has persisted in Christian countries and the racism that has all too often been bred in those countries. While we were able to respond to the global challenge to become teachers of the faith, we did not resist the imperial spirit but allowed it to do very well in Christian circles. The Roman Catholic Church has been international in its membership for all its life and so points to the curious national emphasis in Protestantism, but Rome has been as slow as the rest of us to welcome the true international dimension of theology, liturgy and social witness. It is as though we still find it the most natural thing in the world for white people to dominate the church. The extraordinary spread of Christian faith in the nineteenth century, which was surely part of our obedience to the head of the church, has not fully transformed our perception of what the church is and how it should live. Obedience stops short for most of us at the national boundary.

No doubt God will teach us, but we are slow learners. How significant that it has been left to Live Aid and Sport Aid to demonstrate a truly international effort to meet an international crisis, that our hospitals and universities are often more fully international than our churches, and that the combined weight of United Kingdom churches has failed to persuade the government to act with the international community in such matters as development aid and policy towards South Africa. The church as the body of Christ has been a sluggish, unresponsive body in too many situations of the global village.

The other aspect of change in the human condition that has called for acute listening by the church has been the enormous increase in the power of people to shape the natural environment. This has posed very difficult questions of social morality. We can no longer take for granted that the dominance of the human species can serve the long-term good of all. When the farmer could chop down a few trees for firewood from a forest we could believe that the trees were a gift of God for our use, but when the forest is itself killed by defoliants or acid rain or bulldozers, then we have to question our relationship of mastery. When the master of the natural world has the limited vision or the prejudice or the folly and pride that are part of the human character, who will suffer? The head of the church surely seeks our obedience in such a vital matter for the future, but we tend to push it out of the church agenda as too difficult, too argumentative for our discussion. When we press the question about nuclear energy and nuclear weapons, we expose one of the nerves of the scientific evolution of our era and our uneasiness increases. 'That is too political for our church meeting, it will divide the membership,' we say.

If we followed a dead Christ that might be sufficient response, for he gave no instructions about nuclear physics. But if Christ is alive then his concern for his world must include such life-and-death issues, and our business in the church is constantly to seek his will and to live it out. We know that this does not mean an easy unanimity. It also means that we are not afraid of the hard questions, for our allegiance to Christ is precisely what is given by the Spirit to overcome our differences of view. The obedient body acts in response to its head, and such obedience will include the traditional acts of charity as well as discovery of new ways of facing the urgent opportunities and dilemmas of our generation. Our record is not a great success story.

The next word I suggest for the body-head relationship is expression or expressiveness. It is through the body that the heart and the brain express all that is there, the body is the agent of communication. Our look, our touch, our words, our smile convey the many messages we want to share. Or fail to do so. It often happens that our shyness or clumsiness or inarticulate mumbling hides what we want to tell. The same is true of the church as the body of

Christ. The living Christ speaks, longs to speak, and the church expresses that voice. We are given many kinds of speech. Among the more universal are music, hymns and songs, the architecture of church buildings and their location, the style of life of the members and church leaders, the shape of public worship – all that before we come to the message we preach. We cannot neglect any of the means of communication, but must recognize that we do not all have all the gifts. The body contains a variety of organs, as Paul said, and one of the joys of fellowship is to know that others can display gifts we lack. Our risk is often to limit the range of talents used to share the message of God's grace in Christ, when we stand in urgent need of every possible means of communication. While we encourage drama groups and local broadcasting, we often forget the expression that we show by the physical presence of the church building. Every day I pass one of our churches that was built in the 1950s. It has a severely plain brick frontage on to the street with one high window in frosted glass and a plain locked front door. Its message is 'Fort Knox of religion' or 'Institutional Christianity with a grim face'. I contrast that with a city church I visited in Stockholm where the entry was all light and glass and greenery and a coffee bar. It said, 'We're alive, open, and making city life brighter.' In past ages the building of churches was planned as a sermon in stone, telling the story of Christ, but today the economic functionalism of our architecture renders most of our church buildings silent.

Perhaps music is a stronger language for us. There has certainly been a growth of new hymnody in the last twenty-five years, so that we can sing in contemporary words. It is a joy to hear some of the great choirs as they remind us of beauty and truth in the service of the Word.

For many smaller congregations it is not easy to develop a good musical tradition which speaks the faith and draws others to hear. Simplicity seems to me one of the key words, and that is why the negro spiritual and the Salvation Army song have lasted longer and have spoken more widely than many hymns of much deeper thought. But those with gifts in music or art or drama will set their own standards of truth and devotion so that the Christian community is never satisfied with what is of poor quality. I believe that one of the most constructive audits for a local congregation is to write down all the gifts of communication that are within the membership, and then to see how the gifts may be fully and effectively used. We may be surprised at the range of talent. So it is not all the preacher's work.

Can we be sure what the living Christ is saying, or do we have to dodge between opinions like a baffled voter at election time? We can have absolute confidence in the consistency of Christ. The head of the church is always speaking the word of forgiveness and self-offering, of generosity, of acceptance for the humble, of warning to the pompous and of obedience to the loving heart of God. The body, in all its languages, has to express those ancient words in the most vivid, stirring and joyful forms that are available. This means a major act of translation. Our culture today is so far removed from that of the first disciples that we need courage and freedom to put the same apostolic message into contemporary language. That is the preacher's gift, and that demands the dedication of the congregation too.

My third word is movement. I do not see how the body of Christ can do his will in the world unless it is able to move in response to his will. The great commission was about going, not about standing still. God did not replace Jesus Christ with a statue. The church was called into being in order to carry the Christ-life into every area of human life. At some points of human history this movement has been plain – the evangelization of the tribes of Britain and of northern Europe, the movement of Christians into north Africa, the later global ministries and the translation of the Bible into many languages; these are familiar and reassuring signs of movement. It is right to recall that the static church has also been familiar. It has been static by conviction in many places. When we see the gift of God in Christ as a once-for-all action and the apostolic teaching as the prime authority and the practice of the early church as the one model for church life, and when, in addition, we regard the local church as the permanent sign of the way to eternal life (and all those convictions are not to be despised) then we may expect that a very static form of church will result. I think of this as particularly a gift of Orthodox tradition. It is a way of understanding the church which has revealed extraordinary staying power in adverse circumstances. We have not yet fully appreciated the faithful witness of the Russian church, particularly in the first generation following the Revolution, which kept the call of God before a people caught up in a frightening, chaotic period of change. So the static view of churchmanship demands respect. I still claim that movement is necessary too. Today it may not always be geographical, for the boundaries between the community of faith and the unbelieving world are not readily drawn on any map. That simplicity has gone. Those who today try to excite the church with that geographical theme ('the frontier is over there') are extending a past to comfort our uncertain present.

But movement in the Gospels is towards the point of greatest human need. The body of Christ must always be able to go to that point with its best resources. If there are people homeless in cold cities, then the church will go there to be with them. If there are dying people in hospitals who fear the dark, and angry people in homes divided by human betrayal, and morally blind people in senior military responsibility, and poisoned people waving the flag of racism, and desperate people scratching in the dust for an edible root – then in the form of Christian witness, service, understanding and self-giving the church will move to that focus of need. If this sounds obvious we only have to look at ourselves to know that there is nothing obvious about it. It is far easier for the church to enjoy a static life which says, 'Let the needy come to us.' We probably say that by the very solidity of our property from which we cannot escape. We must not say it by our lives or our ministries. The church is people, and that body can move from the traditional enclosed, private discipleship which is English to the core, to a more mobile and social enterprise. We may thank the Christians from Africa and the Caribbean who are revealing this in our cities today. The body must move.

What does unity mean for the body of the living Christ? There are many attempts at an answer. One emphasis is that the necessary unity is the indwelling of the one Spirit. All in whom the Spirit works become part of one body regardless of the various communions or organizations they join. Another emphasis reminds us that the necessary unity is of faith. All who acknowledge and proclaim the same doctrine become one people who show the key Christian realities to the world. A third approach is to emphasize authority. If Christ is the head

of the body, then the organ through which Christ speaks
has authority and all who recognize that become one
fellowship. A fourth emphasis is on the visible ordering
of the church. If there is one body, then as an organization it will have one style of ministry or one budget or
one name or one liturgy. We can see these different
approaches held with great conviction by recognizable
groups of Christians. The clash between these views
makes difficult all our unity discussions, for we come
with rather different aims. For myself, I have not found a
more adequate expression of the meaning of unity than
the one published by the New Delhi Assembly of the
World Council of Churches (1961):

> We believe that the unity which is both God's will and
> his gift to his Church is being made visible as all in each
> place who are baptized into Jesus Christ and confess
> him as Lord and Saviour are brought by the Holy Spirit
> into one fully committed fellowship, holding the one
> apostolic faith, preaching the one Gospel, breaking the
> one bread, joining in common prayer, and having a
> corporate life reaching out in witness and service to all,
> and who are at the same time united with the whole
> Christian fellowship in all places and all ages in such
> wise that ministry and members are accepted by all
> and that all can act and speak together as occasion
> requires for the tasks to which God calls his people.

It is an omnibus of a sentence. But necessarily so, for it
brings together the key factors of unity in the body of
Christ. Here is the headship of Christ, the action of the
Spirit, the unity of faith, and the local/universal aspects
of the church. Because it is so difficult to find our way to
the fulfilment of this vision, many people have become
prepared to settle for less. We now have much talk of

'conciliar fellowship' and 'reconciled diversity' as modes in which some form of our distinctive communions may continue. Certainly diversity must be a characteristic of the body, as Paul makes plain in I Corinthians 12. It is worth noting that the diversity he frequently wrote about was to do with functions and gifts, not with liturgies, styles of government or beliefs. But we say yes to diversity because the creation by God of humanity reveals the most wonderful diversity of culture, style, ambition, skill, beauty, language, and we cannot believe that this is to be lost in the new creation of the church. It is the signs and evidences of unity which have so far baffled us. I believe it is the living Christ who calls us to work at this with love and commitment, so that we may indeed break the one bread and so heal the most damaging of all our disunities. The breaking of the bread is the breaking of the body of Christ. Yes, but the breaking of his body, the church, is not a testimony to salvation. It reveals the human failure to be humble at the Lord's Table and to welcome there all whom Christ welcomes. It testifies to the death of the body. We pray and work that the Lord may more fully rule in his one church on earth, as in heaven.

14

Risen Christ and our Future

What does the resurrection of Christ tell us about ourselves? Was it an event so solitary, so awe-ful, so distant that we are no wiser regarding our destiny? I think we need to be realistic enough to say that such a case could be made out by people with a philosophic type of mind. It might seem like this. The physical life of Jesus was indeed like ours and his body was subject to all the processes of growing up, tiredness, hunger and so on that we know. His blood had the same chemical composition as ours. Yet his entry into this life and his final departure from the visible world were utterly unique. If, then, we say that he came from God and returned to God in ways that are open to none of us, we may also say that the resurrection and the appearances that followed were part of that divine presence, not to be confused with the human existence of Jesus. And if that is so, then we can deduce nothing from that narrative about ourselves, but can only relate our lives to the period from the Bethlehem stable to the Calvary cross.

I do not believe that is an adequate argument. It is certainly not the understanding of the apostles. But it should not be too easily brushed aside. We do not see the inspired followers of Christ, even those closer to him, risen from their tombs and ascended into heaven. There is no biblical evidence whatever that something like this happened at the end of the earthly life of Mary the mother of Jesus, though some Christians have a strong belief that it was so. Nor do we have such unequivocal messages 'from the other side' to prove to us some continuing existence for those whose earthly life has plainly and conclusively ended. In affirming the bond between the resurrection of Jesus Christ and ourselves we are talking of faith, not of right.

But that bond is at the heart of the good news of Christ, so we must consider the testimony of the apostles. Here is Peter:

> Praise be to the God and Father of our Lord Jesus Christ, who in his great mercy gave us new birth into a living hope by the resurrection of Jesus Christ from the dead. The inheritance to which we are born is one that nothing can destroy or spoil or wither. It is kept for you in heaven (I Peter 1.3–4).

And John:

> The witness is this: that God has given us eternal life, and that this life is found in his Son. He who possesses the Son has life indeed; he who does not possess the Son of God has not that life (I John 5.11–12).

And, as a short quotation from the much longer testimony of Paul:

> But the truth is, Christ was raised to life – the firstfruits of the harvest of the dead. For since it was a man who brought death into the world, a man also brought resurrection of the dead. As in Adam all men die, so in Christ all will be brought to life (I Corinthians 15.20–22).

In their very distinctive styles (which we might call the preacher, the mystic and the theologian) they affirm the same reality, that the single event of Christ's resurrection is the opening of a door through which the followers of Christ also pass. The apostles understood this as fulfilment of what Jesus had told them in the upper room: 'There are many dwelling places in my Father's house; if it were not so I would have told you; for I am going there to prepare a place for you' (John 14.2). As the explorer, breaking through the mountain chain by an unmapped corridor, enables others of less strength and courage to follow, so the Lord Jesus is the forerunner who passes through the tomb to the life which never dies, enabling those who share his life to share it for ever.

The first emphasis is on the resurrection as evidence that the purpose of God is not to be ended by the fact of death. Only vague intimations of continuing life had touched the thought of the Jewish teachers; there was no confirmation that truly satisfied them. The apostles found themselves in a different country. The evidence was there before their eyes. He was dead and buried, as certainly as any man, but he was walking, talking and eating with them. So whatever of finality there was in the death (and 'It is finished' testifies to some conclusion of Christ's purpose) was not the ending of the story of salvation. There was a beyond-the-grave. And if that is so, then we no longer need to regard the grave as the defeat of life, but rather as the conclusion of that phase of life which is visible.

The thinking of Paul in I Corinthians is very strange to us because we have lost his overpowering sense of human solidarity. I think his words are more at home in the African congregation than in our own. 'As in Adam' the whole of humanity has existed under the shadow of

the finality of death, 'so in Christ' there is a new
possibility for the human race, a bond between the life of
God and our small lives. Paul sees human history
flowing from these two poles, the one governing the
zone of shadow, fear, transience; the other the realm of
hope, assurance, glory. I believe that we can only follow
Paul by developing his imagery, not by insisting on his
historical knowledge. Our knowledge of early human
societies is far broader than was possible for Paul, and so
we know that the expectations of eternity were not
exclusive to a few. Many peoples came to this hope, and
prepared a way for the dead to continue an existence
elsewhere. From Egypt to Sri Lanka and Melanesia, from
the emperor's terra cotta army in China to the immortality myths of Greece, we know of a general hope based
on the value we human beings put on our own lives, and
the special hope of rulers that their influence may not be
at an end. Similarly, we can only read as imgery the
phrase about Adam bringing death to the human race,
for we have no conception of a physical living organism
which has no death. 'As in Adam all die' can only be for
us a vivid description of the solidarity of disobedience.
There is a universal distancing of human life from the
community of self-giving love which Jesus shows to be
the nature of God. It is that distancing which is the death,
or death-wish, of humanity. And it is that distancing
which may yet be our physical death through the selfish
grabbing character of nations, their fear and ambition
and short-sightedness.

'Even so in Christ.' That is the startling word of Paul.
There is in the resurrection of Christ as universal a new
hope, as there was a universal disillusion and sorrow.
And it is not, for Paul, just hope, a wish to live for ever, a
grand dream. Rather it is an experience of union with

Christ which is already, today, beyond the reach of death. As Peter writes, it is not just hope but 'a living hope', a hope grounded within life itself. To be at one with Christ is to be joined to beyond-the-grave.

It has often been pointed out that there is a distinction between the apostolic assurance and the many expectations of other religions regarding immortality. In most cases the hopes have been for the continuance of the soul divorced from its fleshly home. But the resurrection of Christ shows us that 'body' is not to be totally discarded as insignificant or evil; rather, it is to be raised, made new, or, as Paul puts it, will be a spiritual body. That antithesis is an attempt to put into words what is beyond our vision and understanding. The life in Christ is not just a soul-life, but personal life in which the reality of our identity is always present. I will still be I and you will be you if we are in Christ, for he loves and rescues people, not souls. So the link between the resurrection of Christ and ourselves is first that faith in Christ, the union between ourselves and Christ, is a new solidarity of living hope. It is an experience of which we know the beginning and therefore can trust the ending. It is based on the love of Christ and the power of God and the non-finality of death.

The second element is the seriousness of choice and decision. The New Testament repeatedly emphasizes that the decisions we make in our lives have an impact far beyond the immediate effects. There are critical choices which affect our life for ever. Say 'No' to the beggar at the gate and you have opened up an unbridgable chasm between your life and the mercy of God. Can it be so? Can we make such determinative choices with so little understanding? Is it not a cruel God who so punishes the careless and the foolish? The key point to note is that the presence of Christ is the presence of God, and Christ is present in the beggar and the hungry and the sick and lonely. Christ is knowable in our world. He comes to us in disguise, in clothes which we would wish to ignore. He is present in the African famine family holding out matchstick arms for a dish of food. And in this way the decisiveness of Christ's presence in one land long ago becomes the very same decisiveness for us today. We cannot escape. It is by the response we make to Christ that we are deciding our eternity, to be with Christ or to be without him. Few of us live sufficiently with this reality, but I find it is a Gospel reality which is undeniable.

So the resurrection of Christ is linked to our future because we have to deal with the living Christ in our world in our day. An objection can certainly be raised at this point. If our conduct towards the poor is our key decision, do we not have a religion of good works which becomes a religion of law? This is a constant struggle within our theology. Everything hinges on faith, we proclaim. There are no good works which can save us. But in the next breath we speak of action, not words; obedience, not prayers. Many great Christians have tried to express this double-sided character of human response to God. I believe that we can only make sense of the duality if in fact it becomes a unity. So long as we separate belief from love we are in an impossible dilemma, and we can end up with Christians who express all the correct beliefs but whose cruelty destroys human life. Or we can end with so flaccid a humanism, so sentimental a charity, that Christ need not have died. Faith, in its full biblical sense, is the whole direction of the personality, the inner priority, the first response and the last confidence, the way of the heart and mind drawn to God in Christ. That cannot exist apart from action. To hear my words and do them, said Jesus, is building on rock. Our ultimate future is determined not by the words we say when we feel religious but by the mercy of God towards the whole direction of our lives.

It is this element in the gospel that preserves our thinking of eternity from becoming the opium that drew the critical fire of Marx. I believe that all too often his critique was justified. Believe, trust in the Lord and you will be safe for ever, so you need not alter life on earth. Master and slave, starving or fat, exploiter or exploited – none of that has any religious importance so long as you believe. That was the ground for socialist criticism. It was necessary medicine. We can be thankful for such a vigorous, painful reminder of the message which came into the world in Jesus. For we see in him that not only does our social conduct matter, but it matters eternally. Each day of our lives brings to us vital choices. This is not to say that we have formal decisions to make every day – whom shall I marry? what profession shall I follow? shall I vote for that new law? shall we emigrate? – the decisions which we know are life-shaping. The strange and humbling reality of the gospel is that the key decisions are small things that pass by unnoticed. Giving a cup of water to a thirsty stranger is not one of those significant decisions for which university education prepares us. Yet it reveals in action where our heart is set. It is a kingdom decision.

The meaning of this for our national and international life is plain. The test of Christ is how we act towards the most hard-pressed of our neighbours, and surely this will be crucial not only for the religious issue of faith but also for the hope of life in this world to come. Christ is alive, and as he addresses us, so he calls for a response. That response shapes the future.

There is another relationship which we celebrate, that of victory. Christus Victor is one of the precious names of Jesus. We are drawn into the victory of Christ, to rejoice in it and to live in the light of it. This was the apostolic trumpet call which survived all the horrors of persecution, which gave peace in the most troubled times, which produced the great songs of faith, which enabled the physically handicapped to live with serenity and which is the only ground we have for confidence in a distressed and divided world. The initiative of God is seen in Christ. The world does its worst. The Lord is risen beyond the cruelty and injustice and disbelief to be with us for ever. Life in that confidence has no time limit.

But there are two other points which press us. The first is, does it matter? If we live this life to the full, use our days and our talents, enjoy God's creation, serve the community and see our place within the story of the generations, then is not this life enough? Why should we hanker for anything more? Christ returned to the Father, the fulfilment of the earthly story and so the fitting last page of the Gospels, but why should that be of great concern to us? My first response is that eternity does not matter to us in the same manner that today does. Indeed, I think there is something rather unhealthy about an eternity-fixation, which we meet in a number of mystics and in some forms of evangelical preaching. It is the most obvious form of religious escapism. I suspect, too, that it is rather like the seeker for happiness who is so concerned with himself that he never knows the great joy of self-forgetfulness. Happiness comes as a gift, never as a target. If our eyes are fixed on what comes after death we shall miss the daily challenges which are God's essential preparation. But there is a deeper level at which this matters. The nature of God and our nature in relation to

God is the background to all our experience of one another. When we human beings exclude the eternal dimension we miss the ultimate significance of life itself, the source from which the value of life comes. For so many people life is 'nasty, brutish and short'. The indignities and corruptions and disappointments of life can turn us all into cynics. The powers of the state and the power of the human brain can seem irresistible. Even the pleasures of our senses, which delight us, can come to defeat us because they are so fleeting. So it is possible to reduce human life to the size of my latest whim or my momentary taste, and then to judge everyone by my satisfaction. We know what happens when a state power is wholly obsessed by its own ideology – other people's lives lose their value. But the background to this life is the life of God. That is the common witness of every part of the Bible. Life matters, the life of every single child, woman and man on earth because each is a gift of God and part of the eternal purpose of God. The resurrection of Jesus Christ affirms this weight of life, this significance.

What about the 'all'? 'So in Christ all will be brought to life,' wrote Paul. How does Christ touch every human life? His influence and grace would appear to be restricted to that section of humanity which has come within the range of the gospel. The apostolic conviction was that the life of Christ was a cosmic event which took place in a small location. Once we come by faith to trust in Jesus as the Son of God, the very life of God in our midst, then we know that the greatest event in history was taking place in that small outpost of empire. Another very surprising 'all' occurs in Colossians 1.23: 'This is the gospel which has been proclaimed in the whole creation under heaven, and I, Paul, have become its minister.' Yet at the time of writing the audible proclamation was by no means universal. The reach of Christ, through resurrection, is beyond our sight and our voices; it is the breadth of the universe. These 'alls' are an affirmation that Christ is ahead of us, beyond us and at work in ways far above our fumbling attempts to share the news about him. The risen Lord is for all. Those various limitations of language and geography no longer bind him, and since his healing purpose remains, we can have confidence that his word of forgiveness and the renewal of human life reach beyond the visible limits of the church. This affirmation is close to the word in John: 'And I shall draw all men to myself when I am lifted up from the earth' (John 12.32). We live in the context of a greater work than we can perceive or imagine.

15

Risen Christ and Returning Christ

During his ministry Jesus looked forward to future events. I suspect that this was partly in response to the typical questioning of all disciples: What is going to happen? We all have this itch to look away from present experience towards the past which we can idolize or criticize without fear of response, or towards the future where our hopes can be realized. It is hard to be content with the present. So it is no surprise that the disciples pressed their master to tell them when the kingdom would arrive in all its glory, and were still occupied with this concept up to the time of the ascension (Acts 1.6). In such a forward look Jesus and the disciples were at one in the use of dramatic images. It was the language of the day. I do not believe we are to take it all with literal understanding about dates or shapes or geography. The Revelation of John, in particular, is far closer to a poetic vision than to Old Moore's Almanack with a chronology.

Yet when we read the Gospels and the Epistles, we cannot help noting that there was a concept of the future coming close and overshadowing human life. A verse in the three Synoptic Gospels records Jesus as announcing: 'There are some standing here who will not taste death before they see the Son of Man coming in his kingdom' (Matthew 16.28; Mark 9.1; Luke 9.27). The nearness of this climax of history was evidently anticipated widely.

We read of Paul's problems with it in I Thessalonians 5, where he urges people to continue with the usual routine of daily life despite what may come. In the Gospels the triumphant return of Christ is associated with the great turmoil of the natural world and of human society, a reign of terror which many have linked with the experience of the destruction of Jerusalem in AD 70. But I think it is inadequate to take particular passages and tie them to secular history and imagine we have done anything useful. There are bigger matters here.

Nor is it sufficient to adopt the position of those who need mathematical certainty. The world has seen too many prophets announcing Armageddon or the Parousia, and the prophets are profitless. If – and we cannot be sure – the word of Jesus about those standing here was spoken as a literal statement of dates, then it was not fulfilled. Since in Acts 1.7 we have a very clear statement from Jesus that, 'It is not for you to know about dates or times, which the Father has set within his own control', it is at least possible that the Synoptic verse had a different intention. But the expectation of an early end certainly shaped much thinking in the apostolic period, and this has tempted many to use all sorts of expertise to uncover the future. Our loss is that we find it very hard to think about the return of Christ in a theological way that will inform our worship and our lives.

The central theme, which is conveyed to us by all the images of the end, is that God contains the whole of history, and that as his will began the process, so his will will conclude it. It is a statement about the nature of God in relation to the world. Whatever freedom is given to the natural processes and the human process, there is no autonomy of a creature within history to start the line or to end it. We may smash a life, bomb a city, kill a tribe, decimate a civilization, but we cannot draw a line under the cosmos. This conviction about the majesty of God is ground for the stability of faith in the midst of darkness. The New Testament witness to Jesus Christ the Son tells us that he is working from the beginning to the end, he is Alpha and Omega, he is one with the Father. That is the context of the return of Christ. Some may see it as an unnecessary piece of mythology which belongs only to the first-century mind, but I would rather look at it as the stone which completes the arch of history.

There is a continuity in God's dealings with the creation, and so we need to find a cohesion and coherence in all the range of Christian doctrine. It is right here that we experience our greatest difficulties with extreme forms of Calvinism, for we cannot hold together the sadism of a God who creates and wills to destruction with the love of a God who offers himself in humility to die for others. In a similar way we find it hard to tie in one bundle an introspective devotion to my own salvation and an activist commitment to social justice. The elastic band of doctrine can be stretched till it snaps. Doctrine, reflecting the way God has shown himself to us, needs consistency. This is the gift of the biblical view of history in the hands of God.

In creation God brings to birth the cosmos in which the community of life is to emerge, the whole varied and beautiful range of life forms which comprise our environment. Humanity is part of that wholeness. It has special gifts and therefore very significant responsibilities. Humanity is set between the animal creation and the divine spirit, touched by both, knowing the limitations of the body and the eternity of inner vision, but still part of the community under God. We draw this understanding of God's purpose both from the creation narratives and

from the experience of Israel and the coming of Jesus.
There is no deviation. The Law was constantly held up
before Israel to bring them into a community life which
reflected the holiness of God. The prophets were at one
in binding together their adoration of God's greatness
and their abhorrence of the social corruption which
disfigured the daily life of Israel. Jesus constantly called
for that response to God which we call love, the greatest
of all the gifts of the Spirit and the life of the Christian
community. Forgiveness is the condition for community
in right relationship to God. So the incarnation can be
seen as God coming to make possible on earth the new
kingdom or community which, in all history, humanity
had battered and mismanaged and trampled on. God
says in Christ: 'Here for you is a new beginning, a new
birth, a new genesis, and it comes through the birth
pains of the cross.' So the doctrine of redemption is
bound to creation, one God, one world, one hope.

It is here that the resurrection surely belongs, for the
Christ who was the word or thought of God in the
beginning comes to the disciples at the moment of their
profound distress to show them that the saving, healing
mission of God continues, transcending the grave, and
will continue. So the statement of faith, that Christ is also
active now and at the end of history, completes the story
from the human point of view. (We cannot pretend to see
our history with the eyes of God.) The conclusion of
creation is the full and complete experience of world
community in God's way, after the pattern of Christ.
Christ, the servant of all, is proclaimed lord of all. So the
kingdom of God, which was present in Jesus himself,
which is experienced in the company of two or three
gathered in Christ's name, and which is to be the
objective of our human search, will be revealed as God's

conclusion. That is the statement of faith, not to be proved by mathematics or textual analysis, but true to all we have seen of the patient, caring, renewing God who gave us life.

The end comes from God. This is why the Revelation of John speaks of the new Jerusalem coming down from heaven, not being built upwards from earth like a supreme tower of Babel. The divine city, described as having jewel-like beauty and everlasting light, is the source of healing streams, as Eden was once described with its four rivers. But the focus of all that is contained in that vision is the Lamb of God. The wounded Lamb in Revelation 5 is the one to break open the seals of God's word, and so to speak all that had been hidden. The word that comes is both wonderful and terrible. But at the end the Lamb means worship and light, for the holy city sees the 'throne of God and of the Lamb' (Revelation 22.3) and in that presence the response can only be a profound worship. After that description John writes:

> Then he said to me, 'These words are trustworthy and true. The Lord God who inspires the prophets has sent his angel to show his servants what must shortly happen. And remember, I am coming soon' (22.6–7).

The nearness of the end is affirmed, and perhaps at that point we catch again the popular apostolic expectation. Christ is to be the divine host, reaper and judge, completing the work of the Holy Spirit within history, fulfilling all that the church was commissioned to do as his body and so effecting at the end the Word spoken in creation. The New Testament offers us visions. Perhaps we should receive them for our prayers and our praise, true for our theology, but not to become entries in next year's diary.

For we commonly have the sense that human history has a far longer time-scale than was evident to the ancients. We have pushed the beginning back far beyond the numbered and named generations of Israel. Similarly the end has been pushed forward by the very lapse of time, but also by what seem to me the signs of immaturity in our human characteristics. Here we touch on the witness of Teilhard de Chardin. How can we think of the present absorption with technology except as a childish concentration on toys, a delight in what we have made and a fear that we may have been too clever? It is all too often Babel in style as well as psychology. Such a concentration on our human fabrications – and we all share it to some extent – suggests to me the immaturity of those who cannot focus on the eternal values. Similarly our human obsession with physical sex is surely part and parcel of the childhood of our race. Both for moralists who have found evil in sex itself, and for sensualists who have made sex their goal, there has been a childish fascination with the physical apparatus. Most of all, however, it is our tribal loyalties that reflect a very childish devotion to the gang. Our international relationships are filled with expressions of self-righteousness (you hit me first, my gang is best) and our parades of authority reflect a very immature pomposity. Racism has all the immaturity of childish fears. So there is ground for regarding our present stage of development as early in the whole story, with far more to come before the creative purpose of God is made clear in the life of humanity. Just as our understanding of geography has given us a much larger map than the biblical authors could imagine, so our glimpse of history has provided a far longer time-scale.

But this is not to persuade us into some facile theory of

progress, as though humanity is on an escalator which will, in time, land us all safely in the booking hall of heaven. Such utopianism has evaporated with the smoke from the chimneys of Auschwitz. Christ is thus not only at work to fulfil the work of creation and redemption, but also to be present as judge. The New Testament is full of images of this. Those who build on sand will have their house swept away when the storm comes. And those (in I Corinthians) who build will have their work tested; 'the day of judgment will expose it'. Or in Hebrews, there is the image of the sabbath rest of the people of God, so 'let us then make every effort to enter that rest, so that no one may fall by following this evil example of unbelief' (4.11). Or there is the harvest image where the weeds, 'whatever makes men stumble, and all whose deeds are evil', are thrown into the furnace (Matthew 13.42). The full exposure of the glory of God means the collapse of all the counterfeit glories of human pride; the light of God's truth throws up the gloomy contrast of our personal propaganda; and the love of God shows up how steadily we have ignored the inner needs of others. So forgiveness alone can unite us with God, and a rejection of that way is death; it is no-hope, the ultimate depression. It is in such terms that I can understand all those old images which often strike us as cruel, and which need to be balanced by the 'all' of the gospel hope. The table of God's feast is open to all; there is sufficient for all; the only negative is that the invitation may be rejected.

Fulfilment and judgment are two of the themes we recognize in the returning Christ. A third is rather more elusive, the combination of patience and hope, the steadfastness of Christ. As the Lord recognized during his ministry that there are no easy routes to a quick

Kingdom triumph, but only the way of the cross, so he
bears with the whole human story and does not dismiss
us. This must surely be one of the most amazing of all
revelations of the nature of God. How many times, and
in how many ways, have we turned our backs on the way
of Christ? Just as the prophets thundered at Israel for
plain disobedience, so there have been proper reasons
for equal thunder in every century of the Christian
church. The cruelties, both great and petty, the narrow
fanaticisms, the careless worship, the mean giving, the
divisions at the Lord's table – we can all assemble a list,
and we know as soon as we write it that we have a share
in the sorrow that we cause for God. And when we turn
to general world history we might readily reach a point of
pessimism that would justify a second flood. But Christ
is alive. He is still working to heal and save. His
invitation is still open as long as human history lasts.
That is the length of God's love, the patience of the
searching shepherd.

So the reality of resurrection and the living Christ is
indeed at the heart of the good news.

The tomb is strong	–	but not final.
The disciples were alone	–	but Jesus came to them.
The Lord was changed	–	but showed he was the same.
His body was scarred	–	and the marks remain.
We do not know him	–	until he reveals himself.
The Spirit reveals him	–	when we least expect it.

Through all the years since the actual event, Christian
people have been finding new courage and new truth in
the living Christ. And the mystery is this: Christ in you,
the hope of a glory to come. So it is this same Christ
whom we picture in an ancient rural simplicity who lives

in the present world in faithful people. We shall meet him at the final welcome and find that we have seen him before. We shall see a victor and know that we met him in that family that grew in love for a disabled child. We shall see a judge and recognize those eyes of a starving beggar. We may touch a hand with scars and remember the pain-love of a mother. For the message of the risen Lord is that he has not been removed for ever from our daily lives, but is closer to us than he was to the first disciples.

To live in this confidence is to begin, in our own circle, another call of the divine community. The final commission in Matthew brought together the word of missionary vocation and the promise of the presence of Christ, and there is no other confidence or technique or programme which can bring the world to the purpose of the creator. For the church throughout the world the only guarantees are in the Christ who is the same yesterday, today and for ever, and not in the forms of church life or the words of doctrinal statements or in our own stumbling pilgrimage. This is precisely the ground for joy and confidence. 'There is no place for human pride in the presence of God. You are in Christ Jesus by God's act' (I Corinthians 1.30). That act has its focus for ever in cross and empty tomb.

Lord Jesus Christ,
you come to us as a brother
with our flesh and blood, our pain and joy;
you come to us as Lord
with the word of absolute challenge
and ultimate assurance;
enable us to greet you
in all who bear your name
in all who carry your scars
and in those who speak your word of life;
so may we live in your presence
as you, by faith, live in us
through the gift of the Holy Spirit
to the glory of God,
for ever.   Amen.